CROCK·POT®

◆ THE ORIGINAL SLOW COOKER ◆

Simple 1-2-3™

Slow Cooker

RECIPES

Publications International, Ltd.

Pictured on front cover: Slow Cooker Cassoulet *(page 57)*.

Pictured on back cover: Burgundy Beef Po' Boys with Dipping Sauce *(page 32)*, Warm Blue Crab Bruschetta *(page 16)*, and Chili Verde *(page 93)*.

ISBN 13: 978-1-4508-0897-2
ISBN 10: 1-4508-0897-2

Library of Congress Control Number: 2010931044

Manufactured in China.

8 7 6 5 4 3 2 1

Contents

Slow Cooking Basics

This fast guide to slow cooking will enhance your experience and your results. You'll wonder how you ever got along without your Crock-Pot® slow cooker.

Stirring

Due to the nature of a slow cooker, there's no need to stir the food unless it specifically says to in your recipe. In fact, taking the lid off to stir food causes the slow cooker to lose a significant amount of heat, extending the cooking time required. Therefore, it's best not to remove the lid for stirring.

Cooking Temperatures and Food Safety

Cooking meats in your **CROCK-POT®** slow cooker is perfectly safe. According to the U.S. Department of Agriculture, bacteria in food are killed at a temperature of 165°F. Meats cooked in the **CROCK-POT®** slow cooker reach an internal temperature in excess of 170°F for beef and as high as 209°F for poultry. It's important to follow the recommended cooking times and to keep the cover on your **CROCK-POT®** slow cooker during the cooking process.

If your food isn't done after 8 hours when the recipe calls for 8 to 10 hours, this could be due to voltage variations, which are commonplace; to altitude; or even to extreme humidity. Slight fluctuations in power don't have a noticeable effect on most appliances; however, they can slightly alter the cooking times. Allow plenty of time, and remember:

It's practically impossible to overcook in a **CROCK-POT®** slow cooker. You'll learn through experience whether to decrease or increase cooking times.

Removable Stoneware

The removable stoneware in your **CROCK-POT®** slow cooker makes cleaning easy. Here are some tips on the use and care of your stoneware:

■ Don't preheat your **CROCK-POT®** slow cooker.

■ Your **CROCK-POT**® slow cooker makes a great server for dips, appetizers, or hot beverages. Keep it on the WARM setting to maintain the proper serving temperature.

■ Because all **CROCK-POT**® slow cookers have wrap-around heat, there is no direct heat from the bottom. For best results, always fill the stoneware at least half full to conform to recommended times. Small quantities can still be cooked, but cooking times will be affected.

Browning Meat

Meat cooked in the **CROCK-POT**® slow cooker will not brown as it would if it were cooked in a skillet or oven at high temperatures. For some recipes, it's not necessary to brown meat before slow cooking. If you prefer the flavor and look of browned meat, however, simply brown the meat in a large skillet coated with nonstick cooking spray before placing it in the stoneware and following the recipe as written.

Adding Ingredients at the End of the Cooking Time

Certain ingredients tend to break down during extended cooking. When possible, add these ingredients toward the end of the cooking time:

■ Milk, cream, and sour cream: Add during the last 15 minutes of cooking time.

■ Seafood: Add in the last 3 to 15 minutes, depending on the thickness and quantity. Gently stir periodically to ensure even cooking.

Cooking for Larger Quantity Yields

Follow these guidelines when preparing recipes in a larger unit, such as a 5-, 6-, or 7-quart **CROCK-POT**® slow cooker:

■ Roasted meats, chicken, and turkey quantities may be doubled or tripled, but seasonings should be adjusted by no more than half. Flavorful seasonings, such as garlic and chili powder, intensify during long, slow cooking. Add just 25 to 50 percent more spices, or as needed to balance flavors.

■ When preparing a soup or a stew, you may double all ingredients except seasonings (see above), dried herbs, liquids, and thickeners. Increase liquid volume by no more than half, or as needed. The **CROCK-POT**® slow cooker lid collects steam, which condenses to keep foods moist and to maintain liquid volume. Don't double thickeners, such as cornstarch, at the beginning. You may always add more thickener later, if needed.

■ When preparing dishes with beef or pork in a larger unit, such as a 5-, 6-, or 7-quart **CROCK-POT**® slow cooker, browning the meat in a skillet before adding it to the stoneware yields the best results; the meat will cook more evenly.

■ When preparing baked goods, it is best not to double or triple the recipe. Simply prepare the original recipe as many times as needed to serve more people.

Spectacular Starts

Chai Tea

- 2 quarts (8 cups) water
- 8 bags black tea
- ¾ cup sugar*
- 16 whole cloves
- 16 whole cardamom seeds, pods removed (optional)
- 5 cinnamon sticks
- 8 slices fresh ginger
- 1 cup milk

Chai tea is typically a sweet drink. For tea that is less sweet, reduce sugar to ½ cup.

1. Combine water, tea, sugar, cloves, cardamom, if desired, cinnamon and ginger in **CROCK-POT®** slow cooker. Cover; cook on HIGH 2 to 2½ hours.

2. Strain mixture; discard solids. (At this point, tea may be covered and refrigerated up to 3 days).

3. Stir in milk just before serving. Serve warm or chilled.

Makes 8 to 10 servings

Triple Delicious Hot Chocolate

3 cups milk, divided
⅓ cup sugar
¼ cup unsweetened cocoa powder
¼ teaspoon salt
¾ teaspoon vanilla
1 cup heavy cream
1 square (1 ounce) bittersweet chocolate
1 square (1 ounce) white chocolate
¾ cup whipped cream
6 teaspoons mini chocolate chips or shaved bittersweet chocolate

1. Combine ½ cup milk, sugar, cocoa and salt in **CROCK-POT®** slow cooker; beat until smooth. Stir in remaining 2½ cups milk and vanilla. Cover; cook on LOW 2 hours.

2. Add cream. Cover; cook on LOW 10 minutes. Stir in bittersweet and white chocolate until melted.

3. Pour hot chocolate into 6 coffee cups. Top each with 2 tablespoons whipped cream and 1 teaspoon chocolate chips.

Makes 6 servings

Spectacular
Starts

Cocktail Meatballs

- **1 pound ground beef**
- **1 pound bulk pork or Italian sausage**
- **1 cup cracker crumbs**
- **1 cup finely chopped onion**
- **1 cup finely chopped green bell pepper**
- **½ cup milk**
- **1 egg, beaten**
- **2 teaspoons salt**
- **1 teaspoon Italian seasoning**
- **¼ teaspoon black pepper**
- **1 cup ketchup**
- **¾ cup packed brown sugar**
- **½ cup (1 stick) butter**
- **½ cup cider vinegar**
- **¼ cup lemon juice**
- **¼ cup water**
- **1 teaspoon yellow mustard**
- **¼ teaspoon garlic salt**

1. Preheat oven to 350°F. Combine beef, sausage, cracker crumbs, onion, bell pepper, milk, egg, salt, Italian seasoning and black pepper in bowl. Mix well; form into 1-inch meatballs. Place on 2 nonstick baking sheets. Bake 25 minutes or until browned.

2. Meanwhile, place ketchup, sugar, butter, vinegar, lemon juice, water, mustard and garlic salt into **CROCK-POT®** slow cooker; mix well. Cover; cook on HIGH until hot.

3. Transfer meatballs to **CROCK-POT®** slow cooker; carefully stir to coat with sauce. Turn to LOW. Cover; cook 2 hours.

Makes 12 servings

Mulled Cranberry Tea

2 tea bags
1 cup boiling water
1 bottle (48 ounces) cranberry juice
½ cup dried cranberries (optional)
⅓ cup sugar
1 large lemon, cut into ¼-inch slices
4 cinnamon sticks
6 whole cloves
Additional cinnamon sticks or thin lemon slices (optional)

1. Place tea bags in **CROCK-POT®** slow cooker. Pour boiling water over tea bags; cover and let stand 5 minutes. Remove and discard tea bags.

2. Stir in cranberry juice, cranberries, if desired, sugar, lemon slices, 4 cinnamon sticks and cloves. Cover; cook on LOW 2 to 3 hours or on HIGH 1 to 2 hours.

3. Remove and discard cooked lemon slices, cinnamon sticks and cloves. Serve in warm mug with cinnamon stick or fresh lemon slice, if desired.

Makes 8 servings

Spectacular Starts

Slow Cooker Cheese Dip

1 **pound ground beef**
1 **pound bulk Italian sausage**
1 **package (16 ounces) pasteurized processed cheese spread, cubed**
1 **can (11 ounces) sliced jalapeño peppers, drained**
1 **medium onion, diced**
8 **ounces Cheddar cheese, cubed**
1 **package (8 ounces) cream cheese, cubed**
1 **container (8 ounces) cottage cheese**
1 **container (8 ounces) sour cream**
1 **can (8 ounces) diced tomatoes, drained**
3 **cloves garlic, minced**
  Salt and black pepper
  Crackers or tortilla chips

1. Brown ground beef and sausage in medium skillet over medium-high heat, stirring to break up meat. Drain and discard fat. Transfer to **CROCK-POT**® slow cooker.

2. Add processed cheese, jalapeño peppers, onion, Cheddar cheese, cream cheese, cottage cheese, sour cream, tomatoes and garlic to **CROCK-POT**® slow cooker. Season with salt and black pepper.

3. Cover; cook on HIGH 1½ to 2 hours or until cheeses are melted. Serve with crackers or tortilla chips.

Makes 16 to 18 servings

·11·
Spectacular Starts

Pizza Fondue

- ½ **pound bulk Italian sausage**
- 1 **cup chopped onion**
- 2 **jars (26 ounces each) meatless pasta sauce**
- 4 **ounces thinly sliced ham, finely chopped**
- 1 **package (3 ounces) sliced pepperoni, finely chopped**
- ¼ **teaspoon red pepper flakes**
- 1 **pound mozzarella cheese, cut into ¾-inch cubes**
- 1 **loaf Italian or French bread, cut into 1-inch cubes**

1. Cook sausage and onion in large skillet until sausage is browned. Drain and discard fat.

2. Transfer sausage mixture to **CROCK-POT®** slow cooker. Stir in pasta sauce, ham, pepperoni and pepper flakes. Cover; cook on LOW 3 to 4 hours.

3. Serve fondue with mozzarella cheese and bread cubes.

Makes 20 to 25 servings

Caponata

1 medium eggplant (about 1 pound), peeled and cut into ½-inch pieces

1 can (about 14 ounces) diced Italian plum tomatoes, undrained

1 medium onion, chopped

1 red bell pepper, cut into ½-inch pieces

½ cup medium-hot salsa

¼ cup extra-virgin olive oil

2 tablespoons capers, drained

2 tablespoons balsamic vinegar

3 cloves garlic, minced

1 teaspoon dried oregano

¼ teaspoon salt

⅓ cup packed fresh basil, cut into thin strips
Toasted sliced Italian or French bread

1. Mix eggplant, tomatoes with juice, onion, bell pepper, salsa, oil, capers, vinegar, garlic, oregano and salt in **CROCK-POT®** slow cooker.

2. Cover; cook on LOW 7 to 8 hours or until vegetables are crisp-tender.

3. Stir in basil. Serve at room temperature on toasted bread.

Makes about 5¼ cups

Spectacular Starts

Mocha Supreme

- **2 quarts strong brewed coffee**
- **½ cup instant hot chocolate beverage mix**
- **1 cinnamon stick, broken into halves**
- **1 cup heavy cream**
- **1 tablespoon powdered sugar**

1. Place coffee, hot chocolate mix and cinnamon stick halves in **CROCK-POT®** slow cooker; stir. Cover; cook on HIGH 2 to 2½ hours or until hot.

2. Remove and discard cinnamon stick halves.

3. Beat cream in medium bowl with electric mixer on high speed until soft peaks form. Add powdered sugar; beat until stiff peaks form. Ladle hot beverage into mugs; top with whipped cream.

Makes 8 servings

Tip: To whip cream more quickly, chill the beaters and bowl in the freezer for 15 minutes.

Honey-Sauced Chicken Wings

3 pounds chicken wings
1 teaspoon salt
½ teaspoon black pepper
1 cup honey
½ cup soy sauce
¼ cup chopped onion
¼ cup ketchup
2 tablespoons vegetable oil
2 cloves garlic, minced
¼ teaspoon red pepper flakes
Toasted sesame seeds (optional)

1. Preheat broiler. Cut off and discard chicken wing tips. Cut each wing at joint to make two sections. Sprinkle with salt and black pepper. Place on broiler pan. Broil 4 to 5 inches from heat 20 minutes or until brown, turning once. Transfer to **CROCK-POT®** slow cooker.

2. For sauce, combine honey, soy sauce, onion, ketchup, oil, garlic and pepper flakes in bowl. Pour over chicken wings.

3. Cover; cook on LOW 4 to 5 hours or on HIGH 2 to 2½ hours. Garnish with sesame seeds, if desired.

Makes about 32 appetizers

Warm Blue Crab Bruschetta

- **4 cups peeled, seeded and diced plum tomatoes**
- **1 cup diced white onion**
- **⅓ cup olive oil**
- **2 tablespoons sugar**
- **2 tablespoons balsamic vinegar**
- **2 teaspoons minced garlic**
- **½ teaspoon dried oregano**
- **1 pound lump blue crabmeat, picked over**
- **1½ teaspoons kosher salt**
- **½ teaspoon cracked black pepper**
- **⅓ cup minced fresh basil**
- **2 baguettes, sliced and toasted**

1. Combine tomatoes, onion, oil, sugar, vinegar, garlic and oregano in **CROCK-POT®** slow cooker. Cover; cook on LOW 2 hours.

2. Add crabmeat, salt and pepper. Stir gently to mix, taking care not to break up crabmeat lumps. Cook on LOW 1 hour.

3. Fold in basil leaves. Serve on toasted baguette slices.

Makes 16 servings

Tip: Crab appetizer also can be served with Melba toast or whole-grain crackers.

Spectacular Starts

Warm and Spicy Fruit Punch

4 cinnamon sticks
1 orange
1 teaspoon whole allspice
½ teaspoon whole cloves
1 square (8 inches) double-thickness cheesecloth
7 cups water
1 can (12 ounces) frozen cranberry-raspberry juice
    concentrate, thawed
1 can (6 ounces) frozen lemonade concentrate, thawed
2 cans (5½ ounces each) apricot nectar

1. Break cinnamon into pieces. Using vegetable peeler, remove strips of orange peel. Squeeze juice from orange; set aside.

2. Rinse cheesecloth; squeeze out water. Wrap cinnamon, orange peel, allspice and cloves in cheesecloth. Tie bag securely with cotton string or strip of cheesecloth.

3. Combine reserved orange juice, water, concentrates and apricot nectar in **CROCK-POT**® slow cooker; add spice bag. Cover; cook on LOW 5 to 6 hours. Remove and discard spice bag before serving.

Makes about 14 servings

Spectacular Starts

Best-Loved Beef

BBQ Beef Sandwiches

- **1 boneless beef chuck roast (about 3 pounds)**
- **¼ cup ketchup**
- **2 tablespoons brown sugar**
- **2 tablespoons red wine vinegar**
- **1 tablespoon Dijon mustard**
- **1 tablespoon Worcestershire sauce**
- **1 clove garlic, crushed**
- **¼ teaspoon salt**
- **¼ teaspoon liquid smoke**
- **⅛ teaspoon black pepper**
- **10 to 12 sandwich rolls or French rolls, sliced in half**

1. Place beef in **CROCK-POT®** slow cooker. Combine remaining ingredients, except rolls, in medium bowl; pour over meat. Cover; cook on LOW 8 to 9 hours.

2. Remove beef from **CROCK-POT®** slow cooker; shred with two forks.

3. Combine beef with 1 cup sauce from **CROCK-POT®** slow cooker. Evenly distribute meat and sauce mixture among warmed rolls.

Makes 10 to 12 servings

Beef with Apples and Sweet Potatoes

1 boneless beef chuck shoulder roast (2 pounds)
1 can (40 ounces) sweet potatoes, drained
2 small onions, sliced
2 apples, cored and sliced
½ cup beef broth
2 cloves garlic, minced
1 teaspoon salt
1 teaspoon dried thyme, divided
¾ teaspoon black pepper, divided
1 tablespoon cornstarch
¼ teaspoon ground cinnamon
2 tablespoons cold water

1. Trim excess fat from beef and discard. Cut beef into 2-inch pieces. Place beef, sweet potatoes, onions, apples, broth, garlic, salt, ½ teaspoon thyme and ½ teaspoon pepper in **CROCK-POT®** slow cooker. Cover; cook on LOW 8 to 9 hours.

2. Transfer beef, sweet potatoes and apples to platter; cover with foil to keep warm. Let cooking liquid stand 5 minutes to allow fat to rise. Skim off fat and discard.

3. Stir together cornstarch, remaining ½ teaspoon thyme, ¼ teaspoon pepper, cinnamon and water until smooth; stir into cooking liquid. Turn **CROCK-POT®** slow cooker to HIGH. Cook 15 minutes until cooking liquid is thickened. Serve sauce with beef, sweet potatoes and apples.

Makes 6 servings

Sloppy Sloppy Joes

- 4 pounds ground beef
- 1 cup chopped onion
- 1 cup chopped green bell pepper
- 1 can (about 28 ounces) tomato sauce
- 2 cans (10¾ ounces each) condensed tomato soup, undiluted
- 1 cup packed brown sugar
- ¼ cup ketchup
- 3 tablespoons Worcestershire sauce
- 1 tablespoon ground mustard
- 1 tablespoon prepared mustard
- 1½ teaspoons chili powder
- 1 teaspoon garlic powder
- Toasted hamburger buns

1. Brown beef in large skillet over medium-high heat, stirring to break up meat. Drain and discard fat.

2. Add onion and bell pepper; cook and stir 5 to 10 minutes or until onion is translucent and mixture is fragrant.

3. Transfer mixture to **CROCK-POT®** slow cooker. Add remaining ingredients, except buns; stir until well blended. Cover; cook on LOW 4 to 6 hours. Serve on buns.

Makes 20 to 25 servings

Dilly Beef Sandwiches

1 **boneless beef chuck roast (3 to 4 pounds)**
1 **jar (6 ounces) sliced dill pickles, undrained**
1 **can (about 14 ounces) crushed tomatoes with Italian seasoning**
1 **medium onion, diced**
4 **cloves garlic, minced**
1 **teaspoon mustard seeds**
  Hamburger buns
  Optional toppings: lettuce, sliced tomatoes, sliced red onions, shredded slaw

1. Trim excess fat from beef and discard. Cut beef into chunks. Place in **CROCK-POT®** slow cooker.

2. Pour pickles with juice over beef. Add tomatoes, onion, garlic and mustard seeds. Cover; cook on LOW 8 to 10 hours.

3. Remove beef from **CROCK-POT®** slow cooker; shred with two forks. Return beef to tomato mixture; mix well. Serve on toasted hamburger buns; top as desired.

Makes 6 to 8 servings

Best-Loved
Beef

Portuguese Madeira Beef Shanks

- **4 cloves garlic, minced**
- **1 large white onion, diced**
- **1 green bell pepper, cored and diced**
- **2 jalapeño peppers, seeded and minced**
- **½ cup diced celery**
- **½ cup minced parsley**
- **4 medium beef shanks, bone in (about 3 pounds total)**
- **1 tablespoon fresh rosemary leaves, minced**
- **1 teaspoon salt**
- **1 cup beef broth**
- **1 cup dry Madeira wine**
- **4 cups hot steamed rice**
- **Horseradish sauce (optional)**

1. Place garlic, onion, bell pepper, jalapeño peppers, celery and parsley in **CROCK-POT**® slow cooker.

2. Rub beef shanks with rosemary and salt. Place shanks on top of vegetables. Pour broth and wine over shanks and vegetables. Cover; cook on LOW 7 to 9 hours.

3. To serve, spoon 1 cup rice into each soup plate. Top rice with beef shank. Spoon vegetable sauce over shanks. Serve with horseradish sauce, if desired.

Makes 4 servings

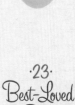

Classic Spaghetti

2 tablespoons olive oil
2 onions, chopped
2 green bell peppers, sliced
2 stalks celery, sliced
4 teaspoons minced garlic
3 pounds lean ground beef
1 can (about 28 ounces) tomato sauce
1 can (28 ounces) stewed tomatoes, undrained
3 cups water
2 carrots, diced
1 cup mushrooms, sliced
2 tablespoons minced parsley
1 tablespoon sugar
1 tablespoon dried oregano
2 teaspoons salt
2 teaspoons black pepper
1 pound uncooked spaghetti

1. Heat oil in large skillet over medium-high heat. Add onion, bell peppers, celery and garlic; cook and stir until tender. Transfer to **CROCK-POT®** slow cooker. In same skillet, brown ground beef. Drain and discard fat; add beef to **CROCK-POT®** slow cooker.

2. Add tomato sauce, tomatoes with juice, water, carrots, mushrooms, parsley, sugar, oregano, salt and black pepper to **CROCK-POT®** slow cooker. Cover; cook on LOW 6 to 8 hours or on HIGH 3 to 5 hours.

3. Cook spaghetti according to package directions; drain. Serve sauce over cooked spaghetti.

Makes 6 to 8 servings

Philly Cheese Steaks

2 pounds beef round steak, sliced
4 onions, sliced
2 green bell peppers, sliced
2 tablespoons butter or margarine, melted
1 tablespoon garlic-pepper seasoning
  Salt, to taste
½ cup water
2 teaspoons beef bouillon granules
8 crusty Italian or French rolls, sliced in half*
8 slices Cheddar cheese, cut in half

*Toast rolls under broiler or on griddle, if desired.

1. Combine beef, onions, bell peppers, butter, garlic-pepper seasoning and salt in **CROCK-POT**® slow cooker.

2. Whisk together water and bouillon in small bowl; pour into **CROCK-POT**® slow cooker. Cover; cook on LOW 6 to 8 hours.

3. Remove beef, onions and bell peppers from **CROCK-POT**® slow cooker and pile on rolls. Top beef with cheese and place under broiler until cheese is melted.

Makes 8 servings

Best-Loved Beef

Hot Beef Sandwiches Au Jus

- 4 pounds beef bottom round roast
- 2 cans (10½ ounces each) condensed beef broth, undiluted
- 1 bottle (12 ounces) beer
- 2 envelopes (1 ounce each) dried onion soup mix
- 1 tablespoon minced garlic
- 2 teaspoons sugar
- 1 teaspoon dried oregano
  Crusty French rolls, sliced in half

1. Trim excess fat from beef and discard. Place beef in **CROCK-POT®** slow cooker.

2. Combine broth, beer, soup mix, garlic, sugar and oregano in large mixing bowl. Pour over beef. Cover; cook on HIGH 6 to 8 hours or until beef is fork-tender.

3. Remove beef from **CROCK-POT®** slow cooker; shred with two forks. Return beef to cooking liquid; mix well. Serve on crusty rolls with extra cooking liquid ("jus") on side for dipping.

Makes 8 to 10 servings

Best-Loved Beef

Slow Cooker Stuffed Peppers

- **1 package (about 7 ounces) Spanish rice mix**
- **1 pound lean ground beef**
- **½ cup diced celery**
- **1 small onion, chopped**
- **1 egg, beaten**
- **4 medium green bell peppers, halved lengthwise, cored and seeded**
- **1 can (28 ounces) whole peeled tomatoes, undrained**
- **1 can (10¾ ounces) condensed tomato soup, undiluted**
- **1 cup water**

1. Set aside seasoning packet from rice. Combine rice mix, beef, celery, onion and egg in large bowl; mix well. Divide meat mixture evenly among bell pepper halves.

2. Pour tomatoes with juice into **CROCK-POT®** slow cooker. Arrange filled bell pepper halves on top of tomatoes.

3. Combine tomato soup, water and reserved rice-mix seasoning packet in medium bowl. Pour over bell peppers. Cover; cook on LOW 8 to 10 hours.

Makes 4 servings

Best-Loved Beef

Slow-Cooked Pot Roast

1 tablespoon vegetable oil
1 beef brisket (3 to 4 pounds)
1 tablespoon garlic powder, divided
1 tablespoon salt, divided
1 tablespoon black pepper, divided
1 teaspoon paprika, divided
5 to 6 new potatoes, cut into quarters
4 to 5 medium onions, sliced
1 pound baby carrots
1 can (about 14 ounces) beef broth

1. Heat oil in large skillet over high heat. Brown brisket on all sides. Transfer brisket to **CROCK-POT®** slow cooker. Season with 1½ teaspoons garlic powder, 1½ teaspoons salt, 1½ teaspoons pepper and ½ teaspoon paprika; set aside.

2. Season potatoes and onions with remaining 1½ teaspoons garlic powder, 1½ teaspoons salt, 1½ teaspoons pepper and ½ teaspoon paprika. Add to **CROCK-POT®** slow cooker.

3. Add carrots and broth to **CROCK-POT®** slow cooker. Cover; cook on HIGH 4 to 5 hours or on LOW 8 to 10 hours or until beef is tender.

Makes 6 to 8 servings

Round Steak

- **1 boneless beef round steak (1½ pounds), trimmed and cut into 4 pieces**
- **¼ cup all-purpose flour**
- **1 teaspoon black pepper**
- **½ teaspoon salt**
- **1 tablespoon vegetable oil**
- **1 can (10¾ ounces) condensed cream of mushroom soup, undiluted**
- **¾ cup water**
- **1 medium onion, quartered**
- **1 can (4 ounces) sliced mushrooms, drained**
- **¼ cup milk**
- **1 package (1 ounce) dry onion soup mix**
- **1 bay leaf**
- **Seasonings, to taste: salt, black pepper, ground sage and dried thyme**

1. Place steak in large resealable food storage bag. Close bag and pound with meat mallet to tenderize steak. Combine flour, 1 teaspoon pepper and ½ teaspoon salt in small bowl; add to bag with steak. Shake to coat meat evenly.

2. Heat oil in large skillet over medium-high heat. Remove steak from bag; shake off excess flour. Add steak to skillet; brown both sides. Transfer steak and pan juices to **CROCK-POT®** slow cooker.

3. Add canned soup, water, onion, mushrooms, milk, soup mix, bay leaf and seasonings to **CROCK-POT®** slow cooker; mix well. Cover; cook on LOW 5 to 6 hours or until steak is tender. Remove and discard bay leaf before serving.

Makes 4 servings

Shredded Beef Fajitas

- 1 beef flank steak (about 1½ pounds)
- 1 can (about 14 ounces) diced tomatoes with green chilies, undrained
- 1 cup chopped onion
- 1 medium green bell pepper, cut into ½-inch pieces
- 2 cloves garlic, minced *or* ¼ teaspoon garlic powder
- 1 package (about 1½ ounces) fajita seasoning mix
- 12 (8-inch) flour tortillas
  Optional toppings: sour cream, guacamole, shredded Cheddar cheese and salsa

1. Cut steak into 6 portions; place in **CROCK-POT®** slow cooker. Combine tomatoes with juice, onion, bell pepper, garlic and fajita seasoning mix in medium bowl. Pour over steak. Cover; cook on LOW 8 to 10 hours or on HIGH 4 to 5 hours or until beef is tender.

2. Remove beef from **CROCK-POT®** slow cooker; shred with two forks. Return beef to **CROCK-POT®** slow cooker and stir.

3. To serve fajitas, place meat mixture evenly into flour tortillas. Add toppings as desired; roll up tortillas.

Makes 12 servings

Classic Beef and Noodles

- 1 tablespoon vegetable oil
- 2 pounds beef stew meat, cut into 1-inch pieces
- ¼ pound mushrooms, sliced into halves
- 2 tablespoons chopped onion
- 2 cloves garlic, minced
- 1 teaspoon salt
- 1 teaspoon dried oregano
- ½ teaspoon black pepper
- ¼ teaspoon dried marjoram
- 1 bay leaf
- 1½ cups beef broth
- ⅓ cup dry sherry
- 1 cup (8 ounces) sour cream
- ½ cup all-purpose flour
- ¼ cup water
- 4 cups hot cooked noodles

1. Heat oil in large skillet over medium heat. Brown beef on all sides. (Work in batches, if necessary.) Drain and discard fat.

2. Combine beef, mushrooms, onion, garlic, salt, oregano, pepper, marjoram and bay leaf in **CROCK-POT**® slow cooker. Pour in broth and sherry. Cover; cook on LOW 8 to 10 hours or on HIGH 4 to 5 hours. Remove and discard bay leaf.

3. Combine sour cream, flour and water in small bowl. Stir about 1 cup cooking liquid from **CROCK-POT**® slow cooker into sour cream mixture. Add mixture to **CROCK-POT**® slow cooker; mix well. Cook, uncovered, on HIGH 30 minutes or until thickened and bubbly. Serve over noodles.

Makes 8 servings

Burgundy Beef Po' Boys with Dipping Sauce

1 boneless beef chuck shoulder or bottom round roast (about 3 pounds)
2 cups chopped onions
¼ cup dry red wine
3 tablespoons balsamic vinegar
1 tablespoon beef bouillon granules
1 tablespoon Worcestershire sauce
¾ teaspoon dried thyme
½ teaspoon garlic powder
Italian rolls, warmed and sliced in half

1. Trim excess fat from beef and discard. Cut beef into 3 or 4 pieces. Place onions on bottom of **CROCK-POT**® slow cooker. Top with beef and remaining ingredients, except rolls. Cover; cook on HIGH 8 to 10 hours or until beef is very tender.

2. Remove beef from **CROCK-POT**® slow cooker; shred beef with two forks. Let cooking liquid stand 5 minutes to allow fat to rise. Skim off fat and discard.

3. Spoon beef into rolls and serve cooking liquid as dipping sauce.

Makes 6 to 8 servings

Osso Bucco

1 large onion, cut into thin wedges
2 large carrots, sliced
4 cloves garlic, sliced
4 meaty veal shanks (3 to 4 pounds)
2 teaspoons herbs de Provence *or* ½ teaspoon each dried
    thyme, rosemary, oregano and basil
1 teaspoon salt
½ teaspoon black pepper
¾ cup canned beef consommé or beef broth
¼ cup dry vermouth (optional)
3 tablespoons flour
¼ cup minced parsley
1 small clove garlic, minced
1 teaspoon grated lemon peel

1. Coat **CROCK-POT®** slow cooker with nonstick cooking spray. Place onion, carrots and sliced garlic in bottom. Arrange veal shanks over vegetables, overlapping slightly, and sprinkle herbs, salt and pepper over all. Add consommé and vermouth, if desired. Cover; cook on LOW 8 to 9 hours or on HIGH 5 to 6 hours, or until shanks and vegetables are tender.

2. Transfer shanks and vegetables to serving platter; cover with foil to keep warm. Turn **CROCK-POT®** slow cooker to HIGH. Combine flour with 3 tablespoons water, mixing until smooth. Stir into cooking liquid. Cover; cook on HIGH 15 minutes or until sauce thickens.

3. Serve sauce over shanks and vegetables. Combine parsley, minced garlic and lemon peel; sprinkle over shanks and vegetables.

Makes 4 servings

Yankee Pot Roast and Vegetables

1 beef chuck pot roast (about 2½ pounds)
   Salt and black pepper
3 unpeeled medium baking potatoes (about 1 pound),
   cut into quarters
2 large carrots, cut into ¾-inch slices
2 stalks celery, cut into ¾-inch slices
1 medium onion, sliced
1 large parsnip, cut into ¾-inch slices
2 bay leaves
1 teaspoon dried rosemary
½ teaspoon dried thyme
½ cup reduced-sodium beef broth

1. Trim excess fat from beef and discard. Cut beef into serving-size pieces; sprinkle with salt and pepper.

2. Combine potatoes, carrots, celery, onion, parsnip, bay leaves, rosemary and thyme in **CROCK-POT®** slow cooker. Place beef over vegetables. Pour broth over beef. Cover; cook on LOW 8½ to 9 hours, or until beef is fork-tender.

3. Transfer beef to serving platter. Arrange vegetables around beef. Remove and discard bay leaves before serving.

Makes 10 to 12 servings

Tip: To make gravy, ladle cooking liquid into 2-cup measure; let stand 5 minutes. Skim off fat and discard. Bring cooking liquid to a boil in small saucepan over medium-high heat. For each cup of cooking liquid, mix 2 tablespoons flour with ¼ cup cold water until smooth. Add to boiling cooking liquid. Cook and stir 1 minute or until thickened.

Spicy Italian Beef

- 1 **boneless beef chuck roast (3 to 4 pounds)**
- 1 **jar (12 ounces) pepperoncini**
- 1 **can (about 14 ounces) beef broth**
- 1 **bottle (12 ounces) beer**
- 1 **onion, minced**
- 2 **tablespoons Italian seasoning**
- 1 **loaf French bread, cut into thick slices**
- 10 **slices provolone cheese (optional)**

1. Trim fat from beef and discard. Cut beef, if necessary, to fit in **CROCK-POT®** slow cooker, leaving beef in as many large pieces as possible.

2. Drain pepperoncini; pull off stem ends and discard. Add next four ingredients to **CROCK-POT®** slow cooker; do not stir. Cover; cook on LOW 8 to 10 hours.

3. Remove beef from **CROCK-POT®** slow cooker; shred with two forks. Return shredded beef to cooking liquid; mix well. Serve on French bread. Top with cheese, if desired. Serve with additional sauce and pepperoncini, if desired.

Makes 8 to 10 servings

Tip: Pepperoncini are small pickled mild peppers. They are available in the supermarket's Italian foods or pickled foods section.

Slow Cooker Brisket of Beef

1 beef brisket (about 5 pounds)
2 teaspoons minced garlic
½ teaspoon black pepper
2 large onions, cut into ¼-inch slices and separated into rings
1 bottle (12 ounces) chili sauce
12 ounces beef broth, dark ale or water
2 tablespoons Worcestershire sauce
1 tablespoon brown sugar

1. Place brisket, fat side down, in **CROCK-POT®** slow cooker. Spread garlic evenly over brisket; sprinkle with pepper. Arrange onions over brisket. Combine chili sauce, broth, Worcestershire sauce and sugar in medium bowl; pour over brisket and onions. Cover; cook on LOW 8 hours.

2. Turn brisket over; stir onions into sauce and spoon over brisket. Cover; cook on LOW 1 to 2 hours or until brisket is fork-tender. Transfer brisket to cutting board; cover with foil to keep warm. Let stand 10 minutes.

3. Stir cooking liquid, then let stand 5 minutes to allow fat to rise. Skim off fat and discard. (Cooking liquid may be thinned to desired consistency with water or thickened by simmering, uncovered, in saucepan.) Carve brisket across grain into thin slices. Spoon cooking liquid over brisket.

Makes 10 to 12 servings

Best-Loved Beef

Curry Beef

1 pound lean ground beef
1 medium onion, thinly sliced
½ cup beef broth
1 tablespoon curry powder
1 teaspoon ground cumin
2 cloves garlic, minced
1 cup (8 ounces) sour cream
½ cup raisins, divided
¼ cup reduced-fat (2%) milk
1 teaspoon sugar
12 ounces uncooked wide egg noodles
¼ cup chopped walnuts, almonds or pecans

1. Brown beef in large skillet over medium-high heat, stirring to break up meat. Drain and discard fat. Add onion, broth, curry powder, cumin, garlic and beef to **CROCK-POT®** slow cooker. Cover; cook on LOW 4 hours.

2. Stir in sour cream, ¼ cup raisins, milk and sugar. Cover; cook on LOW 30 minutes or until thickened and heated through.

3. Cook noodles according to package directions; drain. Serve beef curry over noodles. Sprinkle with remaining ¼ cup raisins and walnuts.

Makes 4 servings

Best-Loved Beef

Beefy Tostada Pie

2 teaspoons olive oil
1½ cups chopped onions
2 pounds ground beef
1 teaspoon chili powder
1 teaspoon ground cumin
1 teaspoon salt
2 cloves garlic, minced
1 can (about 15 ounces) tomato sauce
1 cup sliced black olives
8 flour tortillas
4 cups shredded Cheddar cheese
  Optional toppings: sour cream, salsa and chopped green
  onion

1. Heat oil in large skillet over medium heat. Add onions and cook until tender. Add ground beef, chili powder, cumin, salt and garlic; cook and stir until browned. Stir in tomato sauce; cook until heated through. Stir in black olives.

2. Make foil handles using three 18×2-inch strips of heavy foil, or use regular foil folded to double thickness. Place in **CROCK-POT®** slow cooker; crisscross foil to form spoke design. Lay one tortilla on foil strips. Spread with meat sauce and layer of cheese. Top with another tortilla, meat sauce and cheese. Repeat layers, ending with cheese. Cover and cook on HIGH 1½ hours.

3. To serve, lift out of **CROCK-POT®** slow cooker using foil handles and transfer to serving platter. Discard foil. Cut into wedges. Serve with sour cream, salsa and chopped green onion, if desired.

Makes 4 to 6 servings

Roast Beef Burritos

- **1 boneless beef bottom round roast (3 to 5 pounds)**
- **¼ cup water**
- **½ to 1 teaspoon garlic powder**
- **½ to 1 teaspoon black pepper**
- **1 bay leaf**
- **2 jars (16 ounces each) salsa, plus extra for garnish**
- **2 cans (4 ounces each) diced green chiles, undrained**
- **½ large yellow onion, diced**
- **8 to 10 burrito-size flour tortillas**
- **1 cup shredded Cheddar cheese**

1. Place roast in **CROCK-POT**® slow cooker; add water. Season with garlic powder and pepper. Add bay leaf. Cover; cook on HIGH 6 hours or until beef is tender. Remove and discard bay leaf.

2. Transfer beef to cutting board. Trim fat from beef and discard. Shred beef with two forks. Let cooking liquid stand 5 minutes to allow fat to rise. Skim off fat and discard. Add shredded beef, salsa, chiles and onion to cooking liquid in **CROCK-POT**® slow cooker; stir to combine. Cover; cook on HIGH 1 hour or until onion is tender.

3. To serve, place about 3 tablespoons beef onto each tortilla. Top with cheese and fold into burritos. Place burrito, seam side down, on plate. Microwave 30 seconds to melt cheese. Serve with extra salsa, if desired.

Makes 8 to 10 servings

Seafood Specialties

Creamy Slow Cooker Seafood Chowder

- 1 quart (4 cups) half-and-half
- 2 cans (about 14 ounces each) whole white potatoes, drained and cubed
- 2 cans (10¾ ounces) condensed cream of mushroom soup, undiluted
- 1 bag (16 ounces) frozen hash brown potatoes
- 1 medium onion, minced
- ½ cup (1 stick) butter, cubed
- 1 teaspoon salt
- 1 teaspoon black pepper
- 5 cans (about 8 ounces each) whole oysters, drained and rinsed
- 2 cans (about 6 ounces each) whole baby clams, drained and rinsed
- 2 cans (about 4 ounces each) tiny shrimp, drained and rinsed

1. Combine half-and-half, canned potatoes, soup, frozen potatoes, onion, butter, salt and pepper in **CROCK-POT®** slow cooker; mix well. Cover; cook on LOW 3 to 4 hours.

2. Add oysters, clams and shrimp; stir gently. Cover; cook on LOW 30 to 45 minutes or until seafood is heated through.

Makes 8 to 10 servings

Caribbean Shrimp with Rice

1 package (12 ounces) frozen shrimp, thawed
½ cup chicken broth
1 clove garlic, minced
1 teaspoon chili powder
½ teaspoon salt
½ teaspoon dried oregano
1 cup frozen peas, thawed
½ cup diced tomatoes
2 cups cooked long grain white rice

1. Combine shrimp, broth, garlic, chili powder, salt and oregano in **CROCK-POT®** slow cooker. Cover; cook on LOW 2 hours.

2. Add peas and tomatoes. Cover; cook on LOW 5 minutes. Stir in rice. Cover; cook on LOW 5 minutes longer or until rice is heated through.

Makes 4 servings

Sweet and Sour Shrimp with Pineapple

- **3** cans (8 ounces each) pineapple chunks
- **2** packages (6 ounces each) frozen snow peas, thawed
- **⅓** cup plus 2 teaspoons sugar
- **¼** cup cornstarch
- **2** chicken bouillon cubes
- **2** cups boiling water
- **4** teaspoons soy sauce
- **1** teaspoon ground ginger
- **1** pound medium shrimp, peeled and deveined
- **¼** cup cider vinegar
  Hot cooked rice

1. Drain pineapple chunks, reserving 1 cup juice. Place pineapple and snow peas in **CROCK-POT**® slow cooker.

2. Combine sugar and cornstarch in medium saucepan. Dissolve bouillon cubes in water and add to saucepan. Mix in reserved pineapple juice, soy sauce and ginger. Bring to a boil and cook for 1 minute. Pour into **CROCK-POT**® slow cooker. Cover; cook on LOW 4½ to 5½ hours.

3. Add shrimp and vinegar. Cover; cook on LOW 30 minutes or until shrimp are done. Serve over rice.

Makes 4 servings

Shrimp Jambalaya

1 can (28 ounces) diced tomatoes, undrained
1 medium onion, chopped
1 medium red bell pepper, chopped
1 stalk celery, chopped (about ½ cup)
2 tablespoons minced garlic
2 teaspoons dried parsley flakes
2 teaspoons dried oregano
1 teaspoon hot pepper sauce
½ teaspoon dried thyme
2 pounds cooked large shrimp
2 cups uncooked instant rice
2 cups chicken broth

1. Combine tomatoes with juice, onion, bell pepper, celery, garlic, parsley, oregano, hot pepper sauce and thyme in **CROCK-POT®** slow cooker. Cover; cook on LOW 8 hours or on HIGH 4 hours.

2. Stir in shrimp. Cover; cook on LOW 20 minutes.

3. Meanwhile, prepare rice according to package directions, substituting broth for water. Serve jambalaya over rice.

Makes 6 servings

Seafood
Specialties

Peachy Sweet and Sour Shrimp

- 1 can (about 16 ounces) sliced peaches in syrup, undrained
- ½ cup chopped green onions
- ½ cup chopped red bell pepper
- ½ cup chopped green bell pepper
- ½ cup sliced celery
- ⅓ cup vegetable broth
- ¼ cup light soy sauce
- 2 tablespoons rice wine vinegar
- 2 tablespoons dark sesame oil
- 1 teaspoon red pepper flakes
- 2 tablespoons cornstarch
- ¼ cup water
- 1 package (6 ounces) frozen snow peas, thawed
- 1 pound cooked medium shrimp
- 1 cup cherry tomatoes, cut into halves
- ½ cup toasted walnut pieces
  Hot cooked rice (optional)

1. Place peaches with syrup, green onions, bell peppers, celery, broth, soy sauce, vinegar, sesame oil and pepper flakes in **CROCK-POT®** slow cooker. Cover; cook on LOW 3 to 4 hours or on HIGH 2 to 3 hours or until vegetables are tender. Stir well.

2. Whisk cornstarch into water in small bowl; mix into vegetable mixture. Add snow peas. Cover; cook on HIGH 15 minutes or until thickened.

3. Add shrimp, tomatoes and walnuts. Cover; cook on HIGH 4 to 5 minutes or until shrimp is hot. Serve with rice, if desired.

Makes 4 to 6 servings

Seafood Specialties

Shrimp Creole

¼ cup (½ stick) butter
1 onion, chopped
¼ cup biscuit baking mix
3 cups water
2 cans (6 ounces each) tomato paste
1 cup chopped celery
1 cup chopped green bell pepper
2 teaspoons salt
½ teaspoon sugar
2 bay leaves
   Black pepper, to taste
4 pounds shrimp, peeled, deveined and cleaned
   Hot cooked rice

1. Cook and stir butter and onion in medium skillet over medium heat until onion is tender. Stir in biscuit mix. Place mixture in **CROCK-POT®** slow cooker.

2. Add water, tomato paste, celery, bell pepper, salt, sugar, bay leaves and black pepper. Cover; cook on LOW 6 to 8 hours.

3. Turn **CROCK-POT®** slow cooker to HIGH and add shrimp. Cook 45 minutes to 1 hour or until shrimp are done. Remove bay leaves. Serve over rice.

Makes 8 to 10 servings

Seafood
Specialties

Cream of Scallop Soup

1½ **pounds red potatoes, cubed**
 3 **cups water**
1½ **cups milk**
 2 **onions, chopped**
 2 **carrots, shredded**
 ½ **cup vegetable broth**
 2 **tablespoons white wine**
 ½ **teaspoon garlic powder**
 ½ **teaspoon dried thyme**
 2 **egg yolks, lightly beaten**
 1 **pound sea scallops**
 1 **cup shredded Cheddar cheese**

1. Combine potatoes, water, milk, onions, carrots, broth, wine, garlic powder and thyme in **CROCK-POT®** slow cooker. Cover; cook on LOW 6 to 8 hours or HIGH 3 to 5 hours.

2. Mix in egg yolks. Cover; cook on LOW 1 hour.

3. Add scallops and cook, uncovered, 10 minutes. Mix in cheese and cook, uncovered, 5 minutes or until cheese has melted and scallops are done.

Makes 4 to 6 servings

Tip: Scallops cook very quickly; overcooking will make them tough, so check for doneness early.

Manhattan Clam Chowder

3 slices bacon, diced
3 onions, chopped
2 celery stalks, chopped
2 cups water
1 can (15 ounces) stewed tomatoes, undrained and chopped
4 small red potatoes, diced
2 carrots, diced
½ teaspoon dried thyme
½ teaspoon black pepper
½ teaspoon Louisiana-style hot pepper sauce
1 pound minced clams*

*If minced clams are unavailable, use canned clams. Six 6½-ounce cans yield about 1 pound of clam meat; drain and discard liquid.

1. Cook and stir bacon in medium skillet over medium heat until crisp. Transfer to **CROCK-POT**® slow cooker.

2. Add onions and celery to skillet; cook and stir until tender. Place in **CROCK-POT**® slow cooker. Mix in water, tomatoes with juice, potatoes, carrots, thyme, black pepper and hot pepper sauce. Cover; cook on LOW 6 to 8 hours or HIGH 4 to 6 hours. Add clams during last hour of cooking.

Makes 4 servings

New England Clam Chowder

6 slices bacon, diced
2 onions, chopped
5 cans (6½ ounces each) clams, drained and liquid reserved
6 medium red potatoes, cubed
2 tablespoons minced garlic
1 teaspoon black pepper
2 cans (12 ounces each) evaporated milk
Salt (optional)

1. Cook and stir bacon and onion in medium skillet over medium heat until onions are tender. Place in **CROCK-POT**® slow cooker.

2. Add enough water to reserved clam liquid to make 3 cups. Pour into **CROCK-POT**® slow cooker. Add potatoes, garlic and pepper. Cover; cook on LOW 5 to 8 hours or HIGH 1 to 3 hours.

3. Mix in reserved clams and milk. Cover; cook on LOW 1 hour. Adjust salt to taste, if desired.

Makes 6 to 8 servings

Crowd-Pleasing Pork

Pork and Tomato Ragout

- 2 **pounds pork stew meat, cut into 1-inch pieces**
- ¼ **cup all-purpose flour**
- 3 **tablespoons vegetable oil**
- 2 **pounds red potatoes, cut into ½-inch pieces**
- 1 **can (about 14 ounces) diced tomatoes, undrained**
- 1¼ **cups white wine**
- 1 **cup finely chopped onion**
- 1 **cup water**
- ½ **cup finely chopped celery**
- 2 **cloves garlic, minced**
- ½ **teaspoon black pepper**
- 1 **cinnamon stick**
- 3 **tablespoons chopped fresh parsley**

1. Toss pork with flour in large bowl. Heat oil in large skillet over medium-high heat. Add pork; brown on all sides. Transfer to **CROCK-POT®** slow cooker.

2. Add wine to skillet; bring to a boil, stirring to scrape up browned bits from bottom of skillet. Pour into **CROCK-POT®** slow cooker.

3. Add all remaining ingredients except parsley. Cover; cook on LOW 6 to 8 hours or until pork and potatoes are tender. Remove and discard cinnamon stick. Adjust seasonings, if desired. To serve, sprinkle with parsley.

Makes 6 servings

Scalloped Potatoes and Ham

6 large russet potatoes, sliced into ¼-inch rounds
1 ham steak (about 1½ pounds), cut into cubes
1 can (10¾ ounces) condensed cream of mushroom soup, undiluted
1 soup can water
1 cup shredded Cheddar cheese
Grill seasoning, to taste

1. Layer potatoes and ham in **CROCK-POT®** slow cooker.

2. Combine soup, water, cheese and seasoning in medium bowl. Pour mixture over potatoes and ham.

3. Cover; cook on HIGH 3½ hours or until potatoes are fork-tender. Turn **CROCK-POT®** slow cooker to LOW and cook 1 hour.

Makes 5 to 6 servings

Italian Sausage and Peppers

- 3 cups bell pepper chunks (1 inch), preferably a mix of red, yellow and green*
- 1 small onion, cut into thin wedges
- 3 cloves garlic, minced
- 4 links hot or mild Italian sausage (about 1 pound)
- 1 cup marinara or pasta sauce
- ¼ cup dry red wine
- 1 tablespoon cornstarch
- 1 tablespoon water
  Hot cooked spaghetti
- ¼ cup shredded Parmesan or Romano cheese

Look for mixed bell pepper chunks at supermarket salad bars.

1. Coat **CROCK-POT®** slow cooker with nonstick cooking spray. Place bell peppers, onion and garlic in **CROCK-POT®** slow cooker. Arrange sausage over vegetables. Combine marinara sauce and wine in small bowl; pour over sausage. Cover; cook on LOW 8 to 9 hours on HIGH 4 to 5 hours or until sausage is cooked through and vegetables are very tender.

2. Transfer sausage to serving platter; cover with foil to keep warm. Skim off and discard fat from cooking liquid.

3. Turn **CROCK-POT®** slow cooker to HIGH. Whisk cornstarch into water in small bowl. Stir into cooking liquid. Cook 15 minutes or until sauce has thickened, stirring once. Serve sauce over spaghetti and sausage; top with cheese.

Makes 4 servings

Vegetable-Stuffed Pork Chops

4 double pork rib chops,
   Salt and black pepper
1 can (about 15 ounces) corn, drained
1 green bell pepper, chopped
1 cup Italian-style seasoned dry bread crumbs
1 small onion, chopped
½ cup uncooked converted long grain rice
1 can (8 ounces) tomato sauce

1. Cut pocket into each pork chop, cutting from edge to bone. Lightly season pockets with salt and pepper. Combine corn, bell pepper, bread crumbs, onion and rice in large bowl. Stuff pork chops with rice mixture. Secure open side with toothpicks.

2. Place any remaining rice mixture in **CROCK-POT®** slow cooker. Add stuffed pork chops to **CROCK-POT®** slow cooker. Pour tomato sauce over pork chops. Cover; cook on LOW 8 to 10 hours.

3. Transfer pork chops to serving platter. Remove and discard toothpicks. Serve pork chops with extra rice mixture.

Makes 4 servings

Spicy Asian Pork Filling

- **1 boneless pork sirloin roast (about 3 pounds)**
- **½ cup soy sauce**
- **1 tablespoon chili garlic sauce or chili paste**
- **2 teaspoons minced fresh ginger**
- **2 tablespoons water**
- **1 tablespoon cornstarch**
- **2 teaspoons dark sesame oil**

1. Cut roast into 2- to 3-inch chunks. Combine pork, soy sauce, chili garlic sauce and ginger in **CROCK-POT**® slow cooker; mix well. Cover; cook on LOW 8 to 10 hours or until pork is fork-tender.

2. Remove roast from cooking liquid; cool slightly. Trim excess fat from meat and discard. Shred pork with two forks. Let cooking liquid stand 5 minutes to allow fat to rise. Skim off and discard fat.

3. Turn **CROCK-POT**® slow cooker to HIGH. Blend water, cornstarch and sesame oil in small bowl until smooth; stir into cooking liquid. Cook, uncovered, until thickened. Return pork to **CROCK-POT**® slow cooker; mix well. Cover; cook 15 to 30 minutes or until hot.

Makes 5½ cups filling

Spicy Asian Pork Bundles: Place ¼ cup pork filling into large lettuce leaves. Add shredded carrots, if desired. Wrap to enclose. Makes about 20 bundles.

Mu Shu Pork: Lightly spread prepared plum sauce over small warm flour tortillas. Spoon ¼ cup pork filling and ¼ cup stir-fried vegetables into flour tortillas. Wrap to enclose. Serve immediately. Makes about 20 wraps.

Pork Chops with Jalapeño-Pecan Cornbread Stuffing

6 boneless loin pork chops, 1 inch thick (1½ pounds)
¾ cup chopped onion
¾ cup chopped celery
½ cup coarsely chopped pecans
½ jalapeño pepper, seeded and chopped*
1 teaspoon rubbed sage
½ teaspoon dried rosemary
⅛ teaspoon black pepper
4 cups unseasoned cornbread stuffing mix
1¼ cups reduced-sodium chicken broth
1 egg, lightly beaten

Jalapeño peppers can sting and irritate the skin, so wear rubber gloves when handling peppers and do not touch your eyes.

1. Trim excess fat from pork and discard. Coat large skillet with nonstick cooking spray; heat over medium heat. Add pork; cook 10 minutes or until browned on both sides. Transfer pork to plate.

2. Add onion, celery, pecans, jalapeño pepper, sage, rosemary and black pepper to skillet. Cook 5 minutes or until onion and celery are tender.

3. Combine cornbread stuffing mix, vegetable mixture and broth in medium bowl. Stir in egg. Spoon stuffing mixture into **CROCK-POT®** slow cooker. Arrange pork on top. Cover; cook on LOW about 5 hours or until pork is tender.

Makes 6 servings

Note: For moister dressing, increase chicken broth to 1½ cups.

Slow Cooker Cassoulet

- **1 pound white beans, such as Great Northern beans**
- **1 tablespoon butter**
- **1 tablespoon canola oil**
- **4 veal shanks, 1½ inches thick, tied for cooking**
- **3 cups beef broth**
- **4 ounces maple-smoked bacon or pancetta, diced**
- **3 cloves garlic, smashed**
- **1 sprig each thyme and savory**
   (*or* a bouquet garni of 1 tablespoon each)
- **2 whole cloves**
   Salt and pepper, to taste
- **4 links mild Italian sausages**

1. Rinse and sort beans and place in large bowl; cover completely with water. Soak 6 to 8 hours or overnight. (To quick-soak beans, place beans in large saucepan; cover with water. Bring to a boil over high heat. Boil 2 minutes. Remove from heat; let soak, covered, 1 hour.) Drain beans; discard water.

2. Heat butter and oil in large skillet over medium-high heat until hot. Sear shanks on all sides until browned. Transfer to **CROCK-POT®** slow cooker. Add broth, bacon, garlic, beans, herbs, and cloves. Add enough water to cover beans, if needed. Cover; cook on LOW 8 hours. After about 4 hours, check liquid and add boiling water as needed.

3. Before serving, season with salt and pepper. Grill sausages and serve with cassoulet.

Makes 4 servings

Fall-Off-the-Bone BBQ Ribs

½ **cup paprika**
⅜ **cup sugar**
¼ **cup onion powder**
1½ **teaspoons salt**
1½ **teaspoons black pepper**
2½ **pounds pork baby back ribs, skinned**
1 **can (20 ounces) beer or beef stock**
1 **quart barbecue sauce**
½ **cup honey**
   White sesame seeds and chives for garnish (optional)

1. Preheat grill. Lightly oil grill grate.

2. Meanwhile combine paprika, sugar, onion powder, salt and pepper in small bowl. Generously season ribs with dry rub mixture. Place ribs on grate. Cook for 3 minutes on each side or until ribs have grill marks.

3. Portion ribs into sections of 3 to 4 bones. Place in **CROCK-POT®** slow cooker. Pour beer over ribs. Cover; cook on HIGH 2 hours. Combine barbecue sauce and honey in medium bowl; add to **CROCK-POT®** slow cooker. Cover; cook on HIGH for 1½ hours. Sprinkle with sesame seeds and chives, if desired. Serve with extra sauce on the side.

Makes 6 to 8 servings

Crowd-
Pleasing Pork

Company Slow Cooker Pork Chops

- 2 cans (10¾ ounces each) condensed fat-free cream of mushroom soup, undiluted
- ½ cup skim milk
- 1 package (3 ounces) low-fat cream cheese, softened
- ¼ cup fat-free sour cream
- 2 tablespoons vegetable oil
- 4 to 6 pork loin chops, cut ¾ inch thick
  Black pepper
- 1 jar (2½ ounces) sliced dried beef

1. Blend soup, milk, cream cheese and sour cream until smooth in medium bowl. Heat oil in large skillet over medium-high heat. Brown pork chops on both sides. Season with pepper.

2. Coat **CROCK-POT®** slow cooker with nonstick cooking spray. Place half of pork chops into **CROCK-POT®** slow cooker. Top with 4 slices dried beef. Pour half of sauce mixture over pork. Repeat with remaining chops, dried beef and sauce.

3. Cover; cook on LOW 8 to 9 hours. Adjust seasoning before serving, if necessary.

Makes 4 to 6 servings

Crowd-Pleasing Pork

Sauerkraut Pork Ribs

1 tablespoon vegetable oil
3 to 4 pounds pork country-style ribs
1 large onion, thinly sliced
1 teaspoon caraway seeds
½ teaspoon garlic powder
¼ to ½ teaspoon black pepper
¾ cup water
2 jars (about 28 ounces each) sauerkraut
12 medium red potatoes, quartered

1. Heat oil in large skillet over medium-low heat. Brown ribs on all sides. Transfer to **CROCK-POT®** slow cooker. Drain excess fat and discard.

2. Add onion to skillet; cook until tender. Add caraway seeds, garlic powder and pepper; cook 15 minutes. Transfer onion mixture to **CROCK-POT®** slow cooker.

3. Add water to skillet, stirring to scrape up any browned bits. Pour pan juices into **CROCK-POT®** slow cooker. Partially drain sauerkraut, leaving some liquid; pour over meat. Top with potatoes. Cover; cook on LOW 6 to 8 hours or until potatoes are tender, stirring once during cooking.

Makes 12 servings

Lemon Pork Chops

1 tablespoon vegetable oil
4 boneless pork chops
3 cans (8 ounces each) tomato sauce
1 large onion, quartered and sliced
1 large green bell pepper, cut into strips
1 tablespoon lemon-pepper seasoning
1 tablespoon Worcestershire sauce
1 large lemon, quartered
Lemon wedges (optional)

1. Heat oil in large skillet over medium-low heat. Brown pork chops on both sides. Drain excess fat and discard. Place pork chops into **CROCK-POT®** slow cooker.

2. Combine tomato sauce, onion, bell pepper, lemon-pepper seasoning and Worcestershire sauce, and add to **CROCK-POT®** slow cooker.

3. Squeeze juice from lemon quarters over mixture; drop squeezed peels into **CROCK-POT®** slow cooker. Cover; cook on LOW 6 to 8 hours or until pork is tender. Remove lemon wedges before serving. Serve with additional lemon wedges, if desired.

Makes 4 servings

Crowd-
Pleasing Pork

Poultry in a Pot

Chicken with Italian Sausage

10 ounces bulk mild or hot Italian sausage
6 boneless skinless chicken thighs
1 can (about 15 ounces) white beans, rinsed and drained
1 can (about 15 ounces) red beans, rinsed and drained
1 cup chicken broth
1 medium onion, chopped
1 teaspoon black pepper
½ teaspoon salt
Chopped fresh parsley (optional)

1. Brown sausage in large skillet over medium-high heat, stirring to break up meat. Drain and discard fat. Spoon sausage into **CROCK-POT®** slow cooker.

2. Place chicken, beans, broth, onion, pepper and salt in **CROCK-POT®** slow cooker. Cover; cook on LOW 5 to 6 hours.

3. Adjust seasonings, if desired. Slice each chicken thigh on the diagonal. Serve with sausage and beans. Garnish with parsley.

Makes 6 servings

Old World Chicken and Vegetables

    1 tablespoon dried oregano
    1 teaspoon salt, divided
    1 teaspoon paprika
   ½ teaspoon garlic powder
   ¼ teaspoon black pepper
    2 medium green bell peppers, cut into thin strips
    1 small yellow onion, thinly sliced
    1 cut-up whole chicken (about 3 pounds)
   ⅓ cup ketchup
       Hot cooked egg noodles

1. Combine oregano, ½ teaspoon salt, paprika, garlic powder and black pepper in small bowl; mix well.

2. Place bell peppers and onion in **CROCK-POT®** slow cooker. Add chicken thighs and legs; sprinkle with half of oregano mixture. Add chicken breasts; sprinkle with remaining oregano mixture. Cover; cook on LOW 8 hours or on HIGH 4 hours. Stir in ketchup and remaining ½ teaspoon salt.

3. Serve chicken and vegetables over noodles.

Makes 4 servings

Fresh Herbed Turkey Breast

¼ cup fresh sage, minced
¼ cup fresh tarragon, minced
2 tablespoons butter, softened
1 clove garlic, minced
1 teaspoon black pepper
½ teaspoon salt
1 split turkey breast (about 4 pounds)
1 tablespoon plus 1½ teaspoons cornstarch

1. Combine sage, tarragon, butter, garlic, pepper and salt. Rub mixture all over turkey breast.

2. Place turkey breast in **CROCK-POT®** slow cooker. Cover; cook on LOW 8 to 10 hours or on HIGH 4 to 5 hours or until turkey is no longer pink in the center.

3. Transfer turkey breast to serving platter; cover with foil to keep warm. Turn **CROCK-POT®** slow cooker to HIGH. Slowly whisk cornstarch into cooking liquid cook until thickened and smooth. Slice turkey breast. Serve sauce on the side.

Makes 8 servings

Tip: For 5-, 6- or 7-quart **CROCK-POT®** slow cooker, double all ingredients.

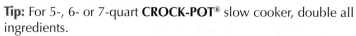

Turkey Tacos

1 **pound ground turkey**
1 **medium onion, chopped**
1 **can (6 ounces) tomato paste**
½ **cup chunky salsa**
1 **tablespoon chopped fresh cilantro**
¾ **teaspoon salt, divided**
1 **tablespoon butter**
1 **tablespoon all-purpose flour**
⅓ **cup milk**
½ **cup sour cream**
   Ground red pepper
8 **taco shells**

1. Brown turkey and onion in large skillet over medium heat, stirring to break up meat. Combine turkey mixture, tomato paste, salsa, cilantro and ½ teaspoon salt in **CROCK-POT®** slow cooker. Cover; cook on LOW 4 to 5 hours.

2. Just before serving, melt butter in small saucepan over low heat. Stir in flour and remaining salt; cook 1 minute. Carefully stir in milk. Cook and stir over low heat until thickened. Remove from heat. Combine sour cream and sprinkle of ground red pepper in small bowl. Stir into milk mixture. Return to heat; cook over low heat 1 minute, stirring constantly.

3. To serve, spoon ¼ cup turkey mixture into each taco shell. Spoon sour cream mixture over taco filling.

Makes 8 tacos

Poultry
in a Pot

Easy Parmesan Chicken

- **8 ounces mushrooms, sliced**
- **1 medium onion, cut in thin wedges**
- **1 tablespoon olive oil**
- **4 boneless skinless chicken breasts**
- **1 jar (26 ounces) pasta sauce**
- **½ teaspoon dried basil**
- **¼ teaspoon dried oregano**
- **1 bay leaf**
- **½ cup (2 ounces) shredded part-skim mozzarella cheese**
- **¼ cup grated Parmesan cheese**
  Hot cooked spaghetti

1. Place mushrooms and onion in **CROCK-POT®** slow cooker.

2. Heat oil in large skillet over medium-high heat. Lightly brown chicken on both sides. Place chicken in **CROCK-POT®** slow cooker. Pour pasta sauce over chicken; add basil, oregano and bay leaf. Cover; cook on LOW 6 to 7 hours or on HIGH 3 to 4 hours or until chicken is tender. Remove and discard bay leaf.

3. Sprinkle chicken with cheeses. Cook, uncovered, on LOW 15 to 30 minutes or until melted. Serve over spaghetti.

Makes 4 servings

Mexican Chili Chicken

2 medium green bell peppers, cut into thin strips
1 large onion, quartered and thinly sliced
4 chicken thighs
4 chicken drumsticks
1 tablespoon chili powder
2 teaspoons dried oregano
1 jar (16 ounces) chipotle salsa
½ cup ketchup
2 teaspoons ground cumin
½ teaspoon salt
  Hot cooked noodles

1. Place bell peppers and onion in **CROCK-POT®** slow cooker; top with chicken. Sprinkle chili powder and oregano evenly over chicken. Add salsa. Cover; cook on LOW 7 to 8 hours or on HIGH 2 to 3 hours or until chicken is tender.

2. Transfer chicken to serving bowl; cover with foil to keep warm. Stir ketchup, cumin and salt into cooking liquid. Cook, uncovered, on HIGH 15 minutes or until hot.

3. Pour mixture over chicken. Serve chicken and sauce over noodles.

Tip: If you prefer a thicker sauce, whisk 1 tablespoon cornstarch into 2 tablespoons water in small bowl. Stir into cooking liquid with ketchup, cumin and salt.

Makes 4 servings

Autumn Chicken

- **1** can (14 ounces) whole artichoke hearts, drained
- **1** can (14 ounces) whole mushrooms, divided
- **12** boneless skinless chicken breasts
- **1** jar (6½ ounces) marinated artichoke hearts, undrained
- **¾** cup white wine
- **½** cup balsamic vinaigrette
- **Hot cooked noodles**
- **Paprika for garnish (optional)**

1. Spread whole artichokes over bottom of **CROCK-POT®** slow cooker. Top with half of mushrooms. Layer chicken over mushrooms. Add marinated artichoke hearts with liquid. Add remaining mushrooms. Pour in wine and vinaigrette.

2. Cover; cook on LOW 4 to 5 hours.

3. Serve chicken and sauce over noodles. Garnish with paprika, if desired.

Makes 10 to 12 servings

Country Captain Chicken

4 **boneless skinless chicken thighs**
2 **tablespoons all-purpose flour**
2 **tablespoons vegetable oil, divided**
1 **cup chopped green bell pepper**
1 **large onion, chopped**
1 **stalk celery, chopped**
1 **clove garlic, minced**
¼ **cup chicken broth**
2 **cups canned crushed tomatoes or diced fresh tomatoes**
½ **cup golden raisins**
1½ **teaspoons curry powder**
1 **teaspoon salt**
¼ **teaspoon paprika**
¼ **teaspoon black pepper**
  Hot cooked rice
  Parsley sprigs (optional)

1. Coat chicken with flour; set aside. Heat 1 tablespoon oil in large skillet over medium-high heat. Add bell pepper, onion, celery and garlic. Cook and stir 5 minutes or until vegetables are tender. Place vegetables in **CROCK-POT**® slow cooker.

2. Heat remaining 1 tablespoon oil in same skillet over medium-high heat. Add chicken; cook 10 minutes or until browned on both sides. Place chicken in **CROCK-POT**® slow cooker.

3. Pour broth into skillet. Cook over medium-high heat, stirring to scrape up any browned bits from bottom of skillet. Pour liquid into **CROCK-POT**® slow cooker. Add tomatoes, raisins, curry powder, salt, paprika and black pepper. Cover; cook on LOW 3 hours. Serve chicken and sauce over rice. Garnish with parsley, if desired.

Makes 4 servings

Chicken Sausage with Peppers & Basil

- **1** tablespoon olive oil
- **½** yellow onion, minced (about ⅓ cup)
- **1** clove garlic, minced
- **1** pound sweet or hot Italian chicken sausage
- **1** can (28 ounces) whole tomatoes, drained and seeded
- **½** red bell pepper, cut into ½-inch slices
- **½** yellow bell pepper, cut into ½-inch slices
- **½** orange bell pepper, cut into ½-inch slices
- **¾** cup chopped fresh basil
  Crushed red pepper flakes, to taste
  Salt and black pepper, to taste
  Hot cooked pasta

1. Heat oil in large skillet over medium heat. Add onion and garlic and cook until translucent.

2. Remove sausage from casing and cut into 1-inch chunks. Add to skillet and cook 3 to 4 minutes, or until just beginning to brown. Transfer to **CROCK-POT®** slow cooker with slotted spoon, skimming off some fat.

3. Add tomatoes, bell peppers, basil, red pepper flakes, salt and black pepper to **CROCK-POT®** slow cooker, and stir to blend. Cook on HIGH 2½ to 3 hours, or until peppers have softened. Adjust seasonings to taste. Serve over pasta.

Makes 4 servings

Tip: It's not necessary to brown meat before slow cooking. However, if you prefer the look and flavor of browned meat, feel free to do so.

Thai Chicken

2½ **pounds chicken pieces**
1 **cup hot salsa**
¼ **cup peanut butter**
2 **tablespoons lime juice**
1 **tablespoon soy sauce**
1 **teaspoon minced fresh ginger**
   Hot cooked rice
½ **cup peanuts, chopped**
2 **tablespoons chopped fresh cilantro**

1. Place chicken in **CROCK-POT®** slow cooker. Combine salsa, peanut butter, lime juice, soy sauce and ginger in small bowl; pour over chicken. Cover; cook on LOW 8 to 9 hours or on HIGH 3 to 4 hours or until done.

2. Serve chicken and sauce over rice; sprinkle with peanuts and cilantro.

Makes 6 servings

Mediterranean Chicken

- **1 tablespoon olive oil**
- **2 pounds boneless skinless chicken breasts**
- **1 can (28 ounces) diced tomatoes, undrained**
- **2 onions, chopped**
- **½ cup dry sherry**
- **2 tablespoons minced garlic**
- **Juice of 2 lemons**
- **2 cinnamon sticks**
- **1 bay leaf**
- **½ teaspoon black pepper**
- **1 pound hot cooked wide noodles**
- **½ cup feta cheese**

1. Heat oil in large skillet over medium heat. Add chicken and lightly brown on both sides.

2. Combine tomatoes with juice, onions, sherry, garlic, lemon juice, cinnamon sticks, bay leaf and pepper in **CROCK-POT®** slow cooker. Add chicken. Cover; cook on LOW 8 to 10 hours or on HIGH 4 to 5 hours or until done.

3. Remove and discard cinnamon sticks and bay leaf. Serve chicken and sauce over noodles. Sprinkle with cheese just before serving.

Makes 6 servings

Moroccan Chicken Tagine

- 3 pounds bone-in chicken pieces, skin removed
- 2 cups chicken broth
- 1 can (about 14 ounces) diced tomatoes, undrained
- 2 onions, chopped
- 1 cup dried apricots, chopped
- 4 cloves garlic, minced
- 2 teaspoons ground cumin
- 1 teaspoon ground ginger
- 1 teaspoon ground cinnamon
- ½ teaspoon ground coriander
- ½ teaspoon ground red pepper
- 6 sprigs fresh cilantro
- 1 tablespoon cornstarch
- 1 tablespoon water
- 1 can (15 ounces) chickpeas, rinsed and drained
- 2 tablespoons chopped fresh cilantro
- ¼ cup slivered almonds, toasted (see tip)
  Hot cooked rice or couscous

1. Place chicken in **CROCK-POT®** slow cooker. Combine broth, tomatoes with juice, onions, apricots, garlic, cumin, ginger, cinnamon, coriander, ground red pepper and cilantro sprigs in medium bowl; pour over chicken. Cover; cook on LOW 4 to 5 hours or until chicken is tender.

2. Transfer chicken to serving platter; cover with foil to keep warm. Whisk cornstarch into water in small bowl until smooth. Stir cornstarch mixture and chickpeas into **CROCK-POT®** slow cooker. Cover; cook on HIGH 15 minutes or until sauce has thickened.

3. Pour sauce over chicken. Sprinkle with chopped cilantro and toasted almonds, and serve over rice.

Makes 4 to 6 servings

Tip: To toast almonds, heat small nonstick skillet over medium-high heat. Add almonds; cook and stir about 3 minutes or until golden brown. Remove from pan immediately. Cool before adding to other ingredients.

Chutney Curried Chicken with Yogurt Sauce

- **1 container (6 to 8 ounces) plain low-fat yogurt**
- **2 teaspoons curry powder**
- **1 teaspoon garlic salt**
- **⅛ teaspoon ground red pepper**
- **4 bone-in chicken breasts, skin removed (2 to 2¼ pounds)**
- **1 small onion, sliced**
- **⅓ cup mango chutney (chop large pieces of mango, if necessary)**
- **1 tablespoon lime juice**
- **2 cloves garlic, minced**
- **2 tablespoons cornstarch**
- **2 tablespoons water**
- **3 cups hot cooked linguine**
- **Optional toppings: chopped fresh cilantro, chopped peanuts or toasted coconut**

1. Place yogurt in paper-towel-lined strainer over a bowl. Drain in refrigerator until serving time.

2. Sprinkle curry powder, garlic salt and ground red pepper over chicken. Place onion in **CROCK-POT®** slow cooker; top with chicken. Combine chutney, lime juice and garlic; spoon over chicken. Cover; cook on LOW 5 to 6 hours or on HIGH 2½ to 3 hours or until chicken is tender.

3. Transfer chicken to serving platter; cover with foil to keep warm. Turn **CROCK-POT®** slow cooker to HIGH. Whisk cornstarch into water in small bowl until smooth. Stir into cooking liquid. Cover; cook 15 minutes or until thickened. Spoon sauce over chicken; serve over linguine. Top with thickened yogurt and garnish as desired.

Makes 4 servings

Poultry in a Pot

Continental Chicken

1 package (2¼ ounces) dried beef, cut into pieces
4 boneless skinless chicken breasts (about 1 pound)
4 slices bacon
1 can (10¾ ounces) condensed cream of mushroom soup, undiluted
¼ cup all-purpose flour
¼ cup reduced-fat sour cream
Hot cooked noodles

1. Coat **CROCK-POT®** slow cooker with nonstick cooking spray. Place dried beef in bottom. Wrap each chicken breast with one bacon slice. Place wrapped chicken on top of dried beef.

2. Combine soup and flour in medium bowl until smooth. Pour over chicken. Cover; cook on LOW 7 to 8 hours or on HIGH 3 to 4 hours.

3. Place sour cream in small bowl; stir in a few tablespoons of cooking liquid from **CROCK-POT®** slow cooker. Stir sour cream mixture into remaining cooking liquid. Cook 5 minutes or until hot. Serve chicken and sauce over noodles.

Makes 4 servings

Creamy Chicken and Mushrooms

- **1 teaspoon salt**
- **½ teaspoon black pepper**
- **¼ teaspoon paprika**
- **3 boneless skinless chicken breasts, cut up**
- **1½ cups sliced mushrooms**
- **½ cup sliced green onions**
- **1¾ teaspoons chicken bouillon granules**
- **1 cup dry white wine**
- **½ cup water**
- **1 can (5 ounces) evaporated milk**
- **5 teaspoons cornstarch**
- **Hot cooked rice**

1. Combine salt, pepper and paprika in small bowl; sprinkle over chicken.

2. Layer chicken, mushrooms, green onions and bouillon in **CROCK-POT®** slow cooker. Pour wine and water over top. Cover; cook on HIGH 3 hours or on LOW 5 to 6 hours. Transfer chicken and vegetables to platter; cover with foil to keep warm.

3. Combine evaporated milk and cornstarch in small saucepan, stirring until smooth. Add 2 cups cooking liquid from **CROCK-POT®** slow cooker; bring to a boil. Boil 1 minute or until thickened, stirring constantly. Serve chicken and sauce over rice.

Makes 3 to 4 servings

Poultry in a Pot

Simple Coq au Vin

4 chicken legs
  Salt and black pepper
2 tablespoons olive oil
½ pound mushrooms, sliced
1 onion, sliced into rings
½ cup dry red wine
½ teaspoon dried basil
½ teaspoon dried thyme
½ teaspoon dried oregano
  Hot cooked rice

1. Season chicken with salt and pepper. Heat oil in large skillet over medium-high heat. Brown chicken on both sides. Transfer chicken to **CROCK-POT®** slow cooker.

2. Add mushrooms and onion to skillet; cook and stir until onions are tender. Add wine, stirring to scrape up any brown bits from bottom of skillet. Add mixture to **CROCK-POT®** slow cooker. Sprinkle with basil, thyme and oregano. Cover; cook on LOW 8 to 10 hours or on HIGH 3 to 4 hours.

3. Serve chicken and sauce over rice.

Makes 4 servings

Poultry in a Pot

Easy Cheesy BBQ Chicken

6 boneless skinless chicken breasts (about 1½ pounds)
1 bottle (26 ounces) barbecue sauce
6 slices bacon
6 slices Swiss cheese

1. Place chicken in **CROCK-POT**® slow cooker. Cover with barbecue sauce. Cover; cook on LOW 8 to 9 hours. (If sauce becomes too thick during cooking, add a little water.)

2. Before serving, cut bacon slices in half. Cook bacon in microwave or on stove top, keeping bacon flat.

3. Turn **CROCK-POT**® slow cooker to HIGH. Place 2 pieces bacon on each chicken breast. Top with cheese slices. Cover; cook until cheese melts.

Makes 6 servings

Savory Soups & Stews

Spicy Cheese Soup

1 pound pasteurized processed cheese product, cubed
1 pound ground beef, cooked and drained
1 can (15 ounces) kidney beans, undrained
1 can (about 14 ounces) diced tomatoes with green chilies, undrained
1 can (about 14 ounces) stewed tomatoes, undrained
1 can (8¾ ounces) whole kernel corn, undrained
1 envelope (about 1 ounce) taco seasoning
1 jalapeño pepper, seeded and diced (optional)
Corn chips (optional)

1. Coat **CROCK-POT®** slow cooker with nonstick cooking spray. Add cheese, beef, beans, tomatoes with chilies, tomatoes with juice, corn, taco seasoning and jalapeño pepper, if desired. Mix well.

2. Cover; cook on LOW 4 to 5 hours or on HIGH 3 hours or until done.

3. Serve with corn chips, if desired.

Makes 6 to 8 servings

Roast Tomato-Basil Soup

2 cans (28 ounces each) peeled whole tomatoes, drained and 3 cups liquid reserved
2½ tablespoons packed dark brown sugar
1 medium onion, finely chopped
3 cups chicken broth
3 tablespoons tomato paste
¼ teaspoon ground allspice
1 can (5 ounces) evaporated milk
¼ cup shredded fresh basil (about 10 large leaves)
Salt and black pepper

1. Preheat oven to 450°F. Line baking sheet with foil; spray with nonstick cooking spray. Arrange tomatoes on foil in single layer. Sprinkle with brown sugar and top with onion. Bake 25 minutes or until tomatoes look dry and light brown. Let tomatoes cool slightly; finely chop.

2. Place tomato mixture, 3 cups reserved liquid from tomatoes, broth, tomato paste and allspice in **CROCK-POT®** slow cooker. Mix well. Cover; cook on LOW 8 hours or on HIGH 4 hours.

3. Add evaporated milk and basil; season with salt and pepper. Cook on HIGH 30 minutes or until hot.

Makes 6 servings

Simmering Hot and Sour Soup

- 2 cans (about 14 ounces each) chicken broth
- 1 cup chopped cooked chicken or pork
- 4 ounces fresh shiitake mushroom caps, thinly sliced
- ½ cup sliced bamboo shoots, cut into thin strips
- 3 tablespoons rice wine vinegar
- 2 tablespoons soy sauce
- 1½ teaspoons chili paste *or* 1 teaspoon hot chili oil
- 4 ounces firm tofu, well drained and cut into ½-inch pieces
- 2 teaspoons sesame oil
- 2 tablespoons cornstarch
- 2 tablespoons cold water
- Chopped cilantro *or* sliced green onions

1. Combine chicken broth, chicken, mushrooms, bamboo shoots, vinegar, soy sauce and chili paste in **CROCK-POT**® slow cooker. Cover; cook on LOW 3 to 4 hours or on HIGH 2 to 3 hours or until done.

2. Stir in tofu and sesame oil. Whisk cornstarch into water in small bowl; stir into soup. Cover; cook on HIGH 10 minutes or until soup has thickened.

3. To serve, sprinkle with cilantro.

Makes 4 servings

Mama's Beer Chili

2 tablespoons olive oil
1 large onion (Vidalia, if available), diced
4 cloves garlic, crushed
1½ to 2 pounds ground turkey
1 can (28 ounces) crushed tomatoes
1 package (10 ounces) frozen corn
1 can (15 ounces) pink beans or kidney beans
1 cup beer (dark preferred)
⅓ cup honey
⅓ cup diced mild green chilies
3 tablespoons chili powder
3 tablespoons hot sauce
3 beef bouillon cubes
1 to 2 tablespoons flour, to thicken
1 teaspoon curry powder

1. Heat oil in large skillet over medium-low heat. Add onion; cook and stir 5 minutes. Add garlic; cook and stir 2 minutes.

2. Add turkey to skillet. Cook and stir until turkey is no longer pink. Drain and discard fat.

3. Add remaining ingredients, stirring until mixed. Transfer to **CROCK-POT®** slow cooker. Cover; cook on LOW 8 to 10 hours or on HIGH 4 to 6 hours.

Makes 4 to 6 servings

Golden Harvest Pork Stew

1 pound boneless pork cutlets, cut into 1-inch pieces
2 tablespoons all-purpose flour, divided
1 tablespoon vegetable oil
2 medium Yukon Gold potatoes, unpeeled and cut into 1-inch cubes
1 large sweet potato, peeled and cut into 1-inch cubes
1 cup chopped carrots
1 ear corn, broken into 4 pieces or ½ cup corn
½ cup chicken broth
1 jalapeño pepper, seeded and finely chopped*
1 clove garlic, minced
1 teaspoon salt
¼ teaspoon black pepper
¼ teaspoon dried thyme
Chopped fresh parsley

*Jalapeño peppers can sting and irritate the skin, so wear rubber gloves when handling peppers and do not touch your eyes.

1. Toss pork pieces with 1 tablespoon flour in large bowl. Heat oil in large skillet over medium-high heat. Add pork; cook until browned on all sides. Transfer to **CROCK-POT®** slow cooker.

2. Add remaining ingredients, except parsley and 1 tablespoon flour. Cover; cook on LOW 5 to 6 hours.

3. Stir ¼ cup cooking liquid into remaining 1 tablespoon flour in small bowl. Stir flour mixture into stew. Turn **CROCK-POT®** slow cooker to HIGH. Cook 10 minutes or until thickened. Adjust seasonings, if desired. To serve, sprinkle with parsley.

Makes 4 servings

Mediterranean Stew

1 medium butternut squash, peeled and cut into 1-inch cubes
2 cups unpeeled eggplant, cut into 1-inch cubes
2 cups sliced zucchini
1 can (15 ounces) chickpeas, rinsed and drained
1 package (10 ounces) frozen cut okra
1 can (8 ounces) tomato sauce
1 cup chopped onion
1 medium tomato, chopped
1 medium carrot, sliced
½ cup vegetable broth
⅓ cup raisins
1 clove garlic, minced
½ teaspoon ground cumin
½ teaspoon ground turmeric
¼ teaspoon ground red pepper
¼ teaspoon ground cinnamon
¼ teaspoon paprika
6 to 8 cups hot cooked couscous or rice
Parsley (optional)

1. Combine all ingredients except couscous in **CROCK-POT®** slow cooker; mix well.

2. Cover; cook on LOW 8 to 10 hours or until vegetables are crisp-tender.

3. Serve over couscous. Garnish with parsley, if desired.

Makes 6 servings

Chili Verde

¾ **pound boneless lean pork, cut into 1-inch cubes**
1 **pound fresh tomatillos, husks removed, rinsed and coarsely chopped**
1 **can (15 ounces) Great Northern beans, rinsed and drained**
1 **can (about 14 ounces) chicken broth**
1 **large onion, halved and thinly sliced**
1 **can (4 ounces) diced mild green chilies**
6 **cloves garlic, chopped or sliced**
1 **teaspoon ground cumin**
   Salt and black pepper, to taste
½ **cup lightly packed fresh cilantro, chopped**

1. Coat large skillet with nonstick cooking spray. Heat over medium-high heat. Add pork; cook until browned on all sides.

2. Combine pork and all remaining ingredients, except cilantro, in **CROCK-POT®** slow cooker. Cover; cook on HIGH 3 to 4 hours.

3. Season to taste with additional salt and pepper. Turn **CROCK-POT®** slow cooker to LOW. Stir in cilantro and cook 10 minutes.

Makes 4 servings

Savory Soups & Stews

Country Sausage and Bean Soup

2 cans (about 14 ounces each) chicken broth
1½ cups hot water
1 cup dried black beans, sorted and rinsed
1 cup chopped onion
2 bay leaves
1 teaspoon sugar
⅛ teaspoon ground red pepper
6 ounces reduced-fat country pork sausage
1 cup chopped tomato
1 tablespoon chili powder
1 tablespoon Worcestershire sauce
2 teaspoons extra-virgin olive oil
1½ teaspoons ground cumin
½ teaspoon salt
¼ cup chopped fresh cilantro

1. Combine broth, water, beans, onions, bay leaves, sugar and ground red pepper in **CROCK-POT®** slow cooker. Cover; cook on LOW 8 hours or on HIGH 4 hours.

2. Coat large skillet with nonstick cooking spray. Heat over medium-high heat. Add sausage and cook until brown, stirring to break up meat.

3. Add sausage and remaining ingredients, except cilantro, to **CROCK-POT®** slow cooker. Cover; cook on HIGH 15 minutes. To serve, sprinkle with cilantro.

Makes 9 servings

Beef Stew with Bacon, Onion and Sweet Potatoes

1 pound beef stew meat, cut into 1-inch chunks
1 can (about 14 ounces) beef broth
2 medium sweet potatoes, peeled and cut into 2-inch chunks
1 large onion, cut into 1½-inch chunks
2 slices thick-cut bacon, diced
1 teaspoon dried thyme
1 teaspoon salt
¼ teaspoon black pepper
2 tablespoons cornstarch
2 tablespoons water

1. Coat **CROCK-POT**® slow cooker with nonstick cooking spray. Combine all ingredients, except cornstarch and water, in **CROCK-POT**® slow cooker; mix well. Cover; cook on LOW 7 to 8 hours or on HIGH 4 to 5 hours, or until meat and vegetables are tender.

2. With slotted spoon, transfer beef and vegetables to serving bowl; cover with foil to keep warm.

3. Turn **CROCK-POT**® slow cooker to HIGH. Whisk cornstarch into water in small bowl. Stir into cooking liquid. Cover; cook 15 minutes or until thickened. To serve, spoon sauce over beef and vegetables.

Makes 4 servings

Chicken and Black Bean Chili

1 pound boneless skinless chicken thighs, cut into 1-inch chunks
2 teaspoons chili powder
2 teaspoons ground cumin
¾ teaspoon salt
1 green bell pepper, diced
1 small onion, chopped
3 cloves garlic, minced
1 can (about 14 ounces) diced tomatoes, undrained
1 cup chunky salsa
1 can (16 ounces) black beans, rinsed and drained
Toppings: sour cream, diced ripe avocado, shredded Cheddar cheese, sliced green onions or chopped cilantro, crushed tortilla or corn chips

1. Combine chicken, chili powder, cumin and salt in **CROCK-POT®** slow cooker, tossing to coat.

2. Add bell pepper, onion and garlic; mix well. Stir in tomatoes with juice and salsa. Cover; cook on LOW 5 to 6 hours or on HIGH 2½ to 3 hours, or until chicken is tender.

3. Turn **CROCK-POT®** slow cooker to HIGH; stir in beans. Cover; cook 5 to 10 minutes or until beans are heated through. Ladle into shallow bowls; serve with desired toppings.

Makes 4 servings

Creamy Cauliflower Bisque

1 pound frozen cauliflower florets
1 pound baking potatoes, peeled and cut in
    1-inch cubes
1 cup chopped onion
2 cans (about 14 ounces each) chicken broth
½ teaspoon dried thyme
¼ teaspoon garlic powder
⅛ teaspoon ground red pepper
1 cup evaporated milk
2 tablespoons butter
½ teaspoon salt
¼ teaspoon black pepper
1 cup shredded sharp Cheddar cheese
¼ cup finely chopped fresh parsley
¼ cup finely chopped green onions

1. Combine cauliflower, potatoes, onion, broth, thyme, garlic powder and red pepper in **CROCK-POT®** slow cooker. Cover; cook on HIGH 4 hours or on LOW 8 hours.

2. Working in batches, place soup in blender and process until smooth, holding blender lid down firmly. Return to **CROCK-POT®** slow cooker. Add evaporated milk, butter, salt and black pepper. Stir until blended and warmed through.

3. To serve, top with cheese, parsley and green onions.

Makes 9 servings

Great Chili

1½ pounds ground beef
1½ cups chopped onion
  1 cup chopped green bell pepper
  2 cloves garlic, minced
  3 cans (15 ounces each) dark red kidney beans, rinsed and drained
  2 cans (15 ounces each) tomato sauce
  1 can (about 14 ounces) diced tomatoes, undrained
  2 to 3 teaspoons chili powder
  1 to 2 teaspoons ground mustard
 ¾ teaspoon dried basil
 ½ teaspoon black pepper
  1 to 2 dried hot chilies (optional)

1. Cook and stir ground beef, onion, bell pepper and garlic in large skillet until meat is browned and onion is tender. Drain fat and discard. Transfer mixture to **CROCK-POT®** slow cooker.

2. Add beans, tomato sauce, tomatoes with juice, chili powder, mustard, basil, black pepper and chilies, if desired; mix well. Cover; cook on LOW 8 to 10 hours or on HIGH 4 to 5 hours.

3. If used, remove chilies before serving.

Makes 6 servings

Potato & Spinach Soup with Gouda

9 **medium Yukon Gold potatoes, peeled and cubed (about 6 cups)**
2 **cans (about 14 ounces each) chicken broth**
½ **cup water**
1 **small red onion, finely chopped**
5 **ounces baby spinach**
½ **teaspoon salt**
¼ **teaspoon ground red pepper**
¼ **teaspoon black pepper**
2½ **cups shredded smoked Gouda cheese, divided**
1 **can (12 ounces) evaporated milk**
1 **tablespoon olive oil**
4 **cloves garlic, cut into thin slices**
5 **to 7 sprigs parsley, finely chopped**

1. Combine potatoes, broth, water, onion, spinach, salt, red pepper and black pepper in **CROCK-POT®** slow cooker. Cover; cook on LOW 10 hours or until potatoes are tender.

2. Slightly mash potatoes in **CROCK-POT®** slow cooker; add 2 cups Gouda and evaporated milk. Cover; cook on HIGH 15 to 20 minutes or until cheese is melted.

3. Heat oil in small skillet over low heat. Cook and stir garlic until golden brown; set aside. Pour soup into bowls. Sprinkle 2 to 3 teaspoons remaining Gouda cheese in each bowl. Place spoonful of garlic in center of each bowl; sprinkle with parsley.

Makes 8 to 10 servings

Minestrone alla Milanese

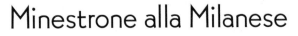

2 cans (about 14 ounces each) beef broth
1 can (about 14 ounces) diced tomatoes, undrained
1 cup diced red potatoes
1 cup coarsely chopped carrots
1 cup coarsely chopped green cabbage
1 cup sliced zucchini
¾ cup chopped onion
¾ cup sliced fresh green beans
¾ cup coarsely chopped celery
¾ cup water
2 tablespoons olive oil
1 clove garlic, minced
½ teaspoon dried basil
¼ teaspoon dried rosemary
1 bay leaf
1 can (15 ounces) cannellini beans, rinsed and drained
Shredded Parmesan cheese (optional)

1. Combine all ingredients except cannellini beans and cheese in **CROCK-POT®** slow cooker; mix well. Cover; cook on LOW 5 to 6 hours.

2. Add cannellini beans. Cover; cook on LOW 1 hour or until vegetables are tender.

3. Remove and discard bay leaf. Garnish with cheese, if desired.

Makes 8 to 10 servings

Vegetarian Chili

- 1 tablespoon vegetable oil
- 1 cup chopped onion
- 1 cup chopped red bell pepper
- 2 tablespoons minced jalapeño pepper*
- 1 clove garlic, minced
- 1 can (28 ounces) crushed tomatoes
- 1 can (15 ounces) black beans, rinsed and drained
- 1 can (15 ounces) chickpeas, rinsed and drained
- ½ cup corn
- ¼ cup tomato paste
- 1 teaspoon sugar
- 1 teaspoon ground cumin
- 1 teaspoon dried basil
- 1 teaspoon chili powder
- ¼ teaspoon black pepper
- Sour cream and shredded Cheddar cheese (optional)

Jalapeño peppers can sting and irritate the skin, so wear rubber gloves when handling peppers and do not touch your eyes.

1. Heat oil in large skillet over medium-high heat. Add onion, bell pepper, jalapeño pepper and garlic; cook and stir 5 minutes or until vegetables are tender. Transfer vegetables to **CROCK-POT®** slow cooker.

2. Add remaining ingredients except sour cream and cheese; mix well. Cover; cook on LOW 4 to 5 hours.

3. Garnish with sour cream and cheese, if desired.

Makes 4 servings

Hearty Veggies & Sides

Spinach Spoon Bread

1   **package (10 ounces) frozen chopped spinach, thawed and squeezed dry**
1   **red bell pepper, diced**
4   **eggs, lightly beaten**
1   **cup cottage cheese**
1   **package (5½ ounces) corn bread mix**
6   **green onions, sliced**
½   **cup (1 stick) butter, melted**
1¼ **teaspoons seasoned salt**

1. Coat **CROCK-POT**® slow cooker with nonstick cooking spray; preheat on HIGH.

2. Combine all ingredients in large bowl; mix well. Pour batter into prepared **CROCK-POT**® slow cooker. Cook, covered, with lid slightly ajar to allow excess moisture to escape, on LOW 3 to 4 hours or on HIGH 1¾ to 2 hours, or until edges are golden and knife inserted in center of bread comes out clean.

3. Loosen edges and bottom with knife and invert onto plate. Cut into wedges to serve. Or, serve bread spooned from **CROCK-POT**® slow cooker.

Makes 8 servings

Winter Squash and Apples

1 **teaspoon salt**
½ **teaspoon black pepper**
1 **butternut squash (about 2 pounds), peeled and seeded**
2 **apples, cored and cut into slices**
1 **medium onion, quartered and sliced**
1½ **tablespoons butter**

1. Combine salt and pepper in small bowl; set aside.

2. Cut squash into 2-inch pieces; place in **CROCK-POT®** slow cooker. Add apples and onion. Sprinkle with salt mixture; stir well. Cover; cook on LOW 6 to 7 hours or until vegetables are tender.

3. Just before serving, stir in butter and season to taste with additional salt and pepper.

Makes 4 to 6 servings

Spanish Paella-Style Rice

2 cans (about 14 ounces each) chicken broth
1½ cups uncooked converted long grain rice
1 small red bell pepper, diced
⅓ cup dry white wine or water
½ teaspoon saffron threads, crushed or
   ½ teaspoon ground turmeric
⅛ teaspoon red pepper flakes
½ cup frozen peas, thawed
   Salt

1. Combine broth, rice, bell pepper, wine, saffron and pepper flakes in **CROCK-POT®** slow cooker; mix well.

2. Cover; cook on LOW 4 hours or until liquid is absorbed.

3. Stir in peas. Cover; cook 15 to 30 minutes or until peas are hot. Season with salt.

Makes 6 servings

Hearty Veggies
& Sides

Scalloped Potatoes and Parsnips

- 6 **tablespoons unsalted butter**
- 3 **tablespoons all-purpose flour**
- 1¾ **cups whipping cream**
- 2 **teaspoons ground mustard**
- 1½ **teaspoons salt**
- 1 **teaspoon dried thyme**
- ½ **teaspoon black pepper**
- 2 **baking potatoes, peeled, cut in half lengthwise, then crosswise into ¼-inch slices**
- 2 **parsnips, cut into ¼-inch slices**
- 1 **onion, chopped**
- 2 **cups (8 ounces) shredded sharp Cheddar cheese**

1. To prepare cream sauce, melt butter in medium saucepan over medium-high heat. Whisk in flour; cook 1 to 2 minutes. Slowly whisk in cream, mustard, salt, thyme and pepper until smooth.

2. Place potatoes, parsnips and onion in **CROCK-POT**® slow cooker. Add cream sauce. Cover; cook on LOW 7 hours or on HIGH 3½ hours or until potatoes are tender.

3. Stir in cheese. Cover; let stand until cheese melts.

Makes 4 to 6 servings

Southwestern Stuffed Peppers

- **4 green bell peppers**
- **1 can (15 ounces) black beans, rinsed and drained**
- **1 cup (4 ounces) shredded pepper jack cheese**
- **¾ cup medium salsa**
- **½ cup frozen corn, thawed**
- **½ cup chopped green onions**
- **⅓ cup uncooked long grain white rice**
- **1 teaspoon chili powder**
- **½ teaspoon ground cumin**
- **Sour cream (optional)**

1. Cut thin slice off top of each bell pepper. Carefully remove seeds, leaving pepper whole.

2. Combine beans, cheese, salsa, corn, onions, rice, chili powder and cumin in medium bowl. Spoon filling evenly into each pepper. Place peppers in **CROCK-POT®** slow cooker.

3. Cover; cook on LOW 4 to 6 hours. Serve with sour cream, if desired.

Makes 4 servings

Hearty Veggies & Sides

Deluxe Potato Casserole

1 can (10¾ ounces) condensed cream of chicken soup, undiluted
1 cup (8 ounces) sour cream
¼ cup plus 3 tablespoons melted butter, divided
¼ cup chopped onion
1 teaspoon salt
2 pounds red potatoes, peeled and chopped
2 cups (8 ounces) shredded Cheddar cheese
1½ to 2 cups stuffing mix

1. Combine soup, sour cream, ¼ cup butter, onion and salt in small bowl.

2. Combine potatoes and cheese in **CROCK-POT®** slow cooker. Pour soup mixture over potato mixture; mix well.

3. Sprinkle stuffing mix over potato mixture; drizzle with remaining 3 tablespoons butter. Cover; cook on LOW 8 to 10 hours or on HIGH 5 to 6 hours or until potatoes are tender.

Makes 8 to 10 servings

Herbed Fall Vegetables

2 medium Yukon Gold potatoes, peeled and cut into ½-inch dice
2 medium sweet potatoes, peeled and cut into ½-inch dice
3 parsnips, peeled and cut into ½-inch dice
1 medium head fennel, sliced and cut into ½-inch dice
½ to ¾ cup chopped fresh herbs, such as tarragon, parsley, sage or thyme
¼ cup (½ stick) butter, cut into small pieces
1 cup chicken broth
1 tablespoon Dijon mustard
1 tablespoon salt
Black pepper

1. Combine potatoes, parsnips, fennel, herbs and butter in **CROCK-POT®** slow cooker.

2. Whisk together broth, mustard, salt and pepper in small bowl. Pour mixture over vegetables.

3. Cover; cook on LOW 4½ hours or on HIGH 3 hours, or until vegetables are tender, stirring occasionally to ensure even cooking.

Makes 6 servings

Mama's Best Baked Beans

1 **bag (1 pound) dried Great Northern beans**
1 **package (1 pound) bacon**
5 **hot dogs, cut into ½-inch pieces**
1 **cup chopped onion**
1 **bottle (24 ounces) ketchup**
2 **cups packed dark brown sugar**

1. Soak and cook beans according to package directions. Drain and refrigerate until ready to use.

2. Cook bacon in large skillet over medium-high heat until crisp. Transfer to paper towels to drain. Cool, then crumble bacon; set aside. Discard all but 3 tablespoons bacon fat from skillet. Add hot dogs and onion. Cook and stir over medium heat until onion is tender.

3. Combine cooked beans, bacon, hot dog mixture, ketchup and brown sugar in **CROCK-POT®** slow cooker. Cover; cook on LOW 2 to 4 hours.

Makes 4 to 6 servings

Cheesy Broccoli Casserole

- **2 packages (10 ounces each) chopped broccoli, thawed**
- **1 can (10¾ ounces) condensed cream of celery soup, undiluted**
- **1¼ cups shredded sharp Cheddar cheese, divided**
- **¼ cup minced onions**
- **½ teaspoon celery seed**
- **1 teaspoon paprika**
- **1 teaspoon hot pepper sauce**
- **1 cup crushed potato chips or saltine crackers**

1. Coat **CROCK-POT®** slow cooker with nonstick cooking spray. Combine broccoli, soup, 1 cup cheese, onions, celery seed, paprika and hot pepper sauce in **CROCK-POT®** slow cooker; mix well.

2. Cover; cook on LOW 5 to 6 hours or on HIGH 2½ to 3 hours or until done.

3. Uncover; sprinkle top with potato chips and remaining ¼ cup cheese. Cook, uncovered, on LOW 30 to 60 minutes or on HIGH 15 to 30 minutes or until cheese melts.

Makes 4 to 6 servings

·III·
Hearty Veggies
& Sides

Corn Bread and Bean Casserole

FILLING
- 1 medium onion, chopped
- 1 medium green bell pepper, diced
- 2 cloves garlic, minced
- 1 can (15 ounces) red kidney beans, rinsed and drained
- 1 can (15 ounces) pinto beans, rinsed and drained
- 1 can (15 ounces) diced tomatoes with green chilies, undrained
- 1 can (8 ounces) tomato sauce
- 1 teaspoon chili powder
- ½ teaspoon ground cumin
- ½ teaspoon black pepper
- ¼ teaspoon hot pepper sauce

TOPPING
- 1 cup yellow cornmeal
- 1 cup all-purpose flour
- 2½ teaspoons baking powder
- 1 tablespoon sugar
- ½ teaspoon salt
- 1¼ cups milk
- 2 eggs
- 3 tablespoons vegetable oil
- 1 can (8½ ounces) cream-style corn, undrained

1. Spray **CROCK-POT®** slow cooker with nonstick cooking spray. Cook onion, bell pepper and garlic in large skillet over medium heat until tender. Transfer to **CROCK-POT®** slow cooker.

2. Stir in beans, tomatoes with chilies, tomato sauce, chili powder, cumin, black pepper and hot pepper sauce. Cover; cook on HIGH 1 hour.

3. Combine cornmeal, flour, baking powder, sugar and salt in large bowl. Stir in milk, eggs and oil; mix well. Stir in corn. Spoon evenly over bean mixture in **CROCK-POT®** slow cooker. Cover; cook on HIGH 1½ to 2 hours or until corn bread topping is done.

Makes 6 to 8 servings

Tip: Spoon any remaining corn bread topping into greased muffin cups; bake 30 minutes at 375°F or until golden brown.

Broccoli and Cheese Strata

- 2 cups chopped broccoli florets
- 4 slices firm white bread, ½ inch thick
- 4 teaspoons butter
- 1½ cups (6 ounces) shredded Cheddar cheese
- 1½ cups low-fat (1%) milk
- 3 eggs
- ½ teaspoon salt
- ½ teaspoon hot pepper sauce
- ⅛ teaspoon black pepper
- 1 cup water

1. Butter 1-quart casserole or soufflé dish that will fit in **CROCK-POT®** slow cooker. Cook broccoli in boiling water 10 minutes or until tender. Drain. Spread one side of each bread slice with 1 teaspoon butter. Arrange 2 slices bread, buttered sides up, in prepared casserole dish. Layer cheese, broccoli and remaining 2 bread slices, buttered sides down.

2. Beat milk, eggs, salt, hot pepper sauce and black pepper in medium bowl. Slowly pour over bread.

3. Place small wire rack in **CROCK-POT®** slow cooker. Pour in 1 cup water. Place casserole on rack. Cover; cook on HIGH 3 hours.

Makes 4 servings

Spicy Beans Tex-Mex

1⅓ cups water
⅓ cup lentils
5 strips bacon
1 onion, chopped
1 can (15 ounces) pinto beans, rinsed and drained
1 can (15 ounces) red kidney beans, rinsed and drained
1 can (about 14 ounces) diced tomatoes, undrained
3 tablespoons ketchup
3 cloves garlic, minced
1 teaspoon chili powder
½ teaspoon ground cumin
¼ teaspoon red pepper flakes
1 bay leaf

1. Combine water and lentils in large saucepan. Boil over medium-high heat 20 to 30 minutes; drain.

2. Cook bacon in medium skillet until crisp. Transfer to paper towels to drain. Cool, then crumble bacon. In same skillet, cook onion in bacon drippings until tender.

3. Combine lentils, bacon, onion, beans, tomatoes with juice, ketchup, garlic, chili powder, cumin, pepper flakes and bay leaf in **CROCK-POT®** slow cooker. Cover; cook on LOW 5 to 6 hours or on HIGH 3 to 4 hours. Remove and discard bay leaf before serving.

Makes 8 to 10 servings

Hearty Veggies & Sides

Risotto-Style Peppered Rice

1 cup uncooked converted long grain rice
1 medium green bell pepper, chopped
1 medium red bell pepper, chopped
1 cup chopped onion
½ teaspoon ground turmeric
⅛ teaspoon ground red pepper (optional)
1 can (about 14 ounces) fat-free chicken broth
4 ounces Monterey Jack cheese with jalapeño peppers, cubed
½ cup milk
¼ cup (½ stick) butter, cubed
1 teaspoon salt

1. Place rice, bell peppers, onion, turmeric and ground red pepper, if desired, in **CROCK-POT®** slow cooker. Stir in broth.

2. Cover; cook on LOW 4 to 5 hours or until rice is tender and broth is absorbed.

3. Stir in cheese, milk, butter and salt; fluff rice with fork. Cover; cook on LOW 5 minutes or until cheese melts.

Makes 4 to 6 servings

Jim's Mexican-Style Spinach

3 packages (10 ounces each) frozen chopped spinach
1 tablespoon canola oil
1 onion, chopped
1 clove garlic, minced
2 Anaheim chilies, roasted, peeled and minced*
3 fresh tomatillos, roasted, husks removed and chopped**
6 tablespoons sour cream (optional)

*To roast chilies, heat heavy skillet over medium-high heat until drop of water sizzles. Cook chilies, turning occasionally with tongs, until blackened all over. Place chilies in brown paper bag for 2 to 5 minutes. Remove chilies from bag and scrape off charred skin. Cut off top and pull out core. Cut lengthwise into halves. With a knife tip, scrape out veins and any remaining seeds.

**To roast tomatillos, heat heavy skillet over medium heat. Leaving papery husks on, cook tomatillos, turning often, until husks are brown and interior flesh is soft, about 10 minutes. When cool enough to handle, remove and discard husks.

1. Place frozen spinach in **CROCK-POT®** slow cooker.

2. Heat oil in large skillet over medium heat until hot. Cook and stir onion and garlic 5 minutes or until onion is soft but not browned. Add chilies and tomatillos; cook 3 to 4 minutes. Add mixture to **CROCK-POT®** slow cooker.

3. Cover; cook on LOW 4 to 6 hours. Stir before serving. Serve with sour cream, if desired.

Makes 6 servings

Pesto Rice and Beans

1 can (15 ounces) Great Northern beans, rinsed and drained
1 can (about 14 ounces) chicken broth
¾ cup uncooked converted long grain rice
1½ cups frozen cut green beans, thawed and drained
½ cup prepared pesto
    Grated Parmesan cheese (optional)

1. Combine Great Northern beans, broth and rice in **CROCK-POT®** slow cooker. Cover; cook on LOW 2 hours.

2. Stir in green beans. Cover; cook 1 hour or until rice and beans are tender.

3. Turn off **CROCK-POT®** slow cooker and transfer stoneware to heatproof surface. Stir in pesto and Parmesan cheese, if desired. Let stand, covered, 5 minutes or until cheese is melted. Serve immediately.

Makes 8 servings

Hearty Veggies
& Sides

Bean and Vegetable Burritos

2 tablespoons chili powder
2 teaspoons dried oregano
1½ teaspoons ground cumin
1 large sweet potato, peeled and diced
1 can (15 ounces) black beans, rinsed and drained
4 cloves garlic, minced
1 medium onion, halved and thinly sliced
1 jalapeño pepper, seeded and minced*
1 green bell pepper, chopped
1 cup frozen corn, thawed and drained
3 tablespoons lime juice
1 tablespoon chopped fresh cilantro
¾ cup (3 ounces) shredded Monterey Jack cheese
4 (10-inch) flour tortillas

Jalapeño peppers can sting and irritate the skin, so wear rubber gloves when handling peppers and do not touch your eyes.

1. Combine chili powder, oregano and cumin in small bowl. Set aside.

2. Layer ingredients in **CROCK-POT®** slow cooker in following order: sweet potato, beans, half of chili powder mixture, garlic, onion, jalapeño pepper, bell pepper, remaining half of chili powder mixture and corn. Cover; cook on LOW 5 hours or until sweet potato is tender. Stir in lime juice and cilantro.

3. Preheat oven to 350°F. Spoon 2 tablespoons cheese into center of each tortilla. Top with 1 cup filling. Fold up bottom edge of tortilla over filling, fold in sides and roll to enclose filling. Place burrito, seam side down, on baking sheet. Repeat with remaining tortillas. Cover with foil and bake 20 to 30 minutes or until heated through.

Makes 4 servings

Hearty Veggies
& Sides

Corn on the Cob
with Garlic Herb Butter

½ cup (1 stick) unsalted butter, softened
3 to 4 cloves garlic, minced
2 tablespoons finely minced fresh parsley
4 to 5 ears of corn, husked
 Salt and black pepper

1. Thoroughly mix butter, garlic and parsley in small bowl.

2. Place each ear of corn on a piece of aluminum foil and generously spread with butter. Season with salt and pepper and tightly seal foil.

3. Place in **CROCK-POT®** slow cooker, overlapping ears if necessary. Add enough water to come one-fourth of the way up each ear. Cover; cook on LOW 4 to 5 hours or on HIGH 2 to 2½ hours or until done.

Makes 4 to 5 servings

Slow-Cooked Sweets

Brownie Bottoms

- ¾ **cup water**
- ½ **cup packed brown sugar**
- 2 **tablespoons unsweetened cocoa powder**
- 2½ **cups packaged brownie mix**
- 1 **package (2¾ ounces) instant chocolate pudding mix**
- ½ **cup milk chocolate chips**
- 2 **eggs, beaten**
- 3 **tablespoons butter or margarine, melted**

1. Lightly coat **CROCK-POT**® slow cooker with nonstick cooking spray. Combine water, brown sugar and cocoa powder in small saucepan; bring to a boil over medium-high heat.

2. Combine brownie mix, pudding mix, chocolate chips, eggs and butter in medium bowl; stir until well blended. Spread batter in bottom of **CROCK-POT**® slow cooker. Pour boiling sugar mixture over batter. Cover; cook on HIGH 1½ hours.

3. Turn off **CROCK-POT**® slow cooker and let stand for 30 minutes. Serve warm with whipped cream or ice cream, if desired.

Makes 6 servings

Tip: For 5-, 6- or 7-quart **CROCK-POT**® slow cooker, double all ingredients.

Mixed Berry Cobbler

1 package (16 ounces) frozen mixed berries
¾ cup granulated sugar
2 tablespoons quick-cooking tapioca
2 teaspoons grated lemon peel
1½ cups all-purpose flour
½ cup packed brown sugar
2¼ teaspoons baking powder
¼ teaspoon ground nutmeg
¾ cup milk
⅓ cup butter, melted
Vanilla ice cream (optional)

1. Stir together berries, granulated sugar, tapioca and lemon peel in **CROCK-POT®** slow cooker.

2. Combine flour, brown sugar, baking powder and nutmeg in medium bowl. Add milk and butter; stir just until blended. Drop spoonfuls of dough on top of berry mixture.

3. Cover; cook on LOW 4 hours. Uncover; let stand about 30 minutes. Serve with ice cream, if desired.

Makes 8 servings

Apple-Date Crisp

6 cups thinly sliced peeled apples
(about 6 medium, preferably Golden Delicious)
2 teaspoons lemon juice
⅓ cup chopped dates
1⅓ cups uncooked quick oats
½ cup all-purpose flour
½ cup packed light brown sugar
½ teaspoon ground cinnamon
¼ teaspoon ground ginger
¼ teaspoon salt
Dash ground nutmeg
Dash ground cloves (optional)
¼ cup (½ stick) cold butter, cut into small pieces

1. Coat **CROCK-POT®** slow cooker with nonstick cooking spray. Place apples in medium bowl. Sprinkle with lemon juice; toss to coat. Add dates and mix well. Transfer mixture to **CROCK-POT®** slow cooker.

2. Combine oats, flour, brown sugar, cinnamon, ginger, salt, nutmeg and cloves, if desired, in medium bowl. Cut in butter with pastry blender or two knives until mixture resembles coarse crumbs.

3. Sprinkle oat mixture over apples; smooth top. Cover; cook on LOW 4 hours or on HIGH 2 hours or until apples are tender.

Makes 6 servings

Coconut Rice Pudding

2 cups water
1 cup uncooked converted long grain rice
1 tablespoon unsalted butter
Pinch salt
2¼ cups evaporated milk
1 can (14 ounces) cream of coconut
½ cup golden raisins
3 egg yolks, beaten
Grated peel of 2 limes
1 teaspoon vanilla
Toasted shredded coconut (optional)

1. Place water, rice, butter and salt in medium saucepan. Bring to a boil over high heat, stirring frequently. Reduce heat to low. Cover; cook 10 to 12 minutes. Remove from heat. Let stand, covered, 5 minutes.

2. Meanwhile, coat **CROCK-POT®** slow cooker with nonstick cooking spray. Add evaporated milk, cream of coconut, raisins, egg yolks, lime peel and vanilla; mix well. Add rice; stir until blended.

3. Cover; cook on LOW 4 hours or on HIGH 2 hours. Stir every 30 minutes, if possible. Pudding will thicken as it cools. Garnish with toasted shredded coconut, if desired.

Makes 6 servings

Slow-Cooked
Sweets

Cran-Apple Orange Conserve

- **2** medium oranges, washed
- **5** large tart apples, peeled, cored and chopped
- **2** cups sugar
- **1½** cups fresh cranberries
- **1** tablespoon grated lemon peel
  Pound cake

1. Remove thin slice from both ends of both oranges for easier chopping. Finely chop unpeeled oranges and remove any seeds to yield about 2 cups of chopped oranges.

2. Combine chopped oranges, apples, sugar, cranberries and lemon peel in **CROCK-POT®** slow cooker. Cover; cook on LOW 4 hours or on HIGH 2 hours.

3. Slightly crush fruit with potato masher. Cook, uncovered, on LOW 2 hours or on HIGH 1 to 1½ hours or until very thick, stirring occasionally to prevent sticking. Cool at least 2 hours. Serve over pound cake.

Makes about 5 cups

Fruit Ambrosia with Dumplings

  4 cups fresh or frozen fruit*
 ½ cup plus 2 tablespoons granulated sugar, divided
 ½ cup warm apple or cran-apple juice
  2 tablespoons quick-cooking tapioca
  1 cup all-purpose flour
1¼ teaspoons baking powder
 ¼ teaspoon salt
  3 tablespoons butter, cut into small pieces
 ½ cup milk
  1 egg
  2 tablespoons light brown sugar, plus additional
    for garnish
    Ice cream, sweetened whipped cream or yogurt (optional)

Use strawberries, raspberries, blueberries or peaches.

1. Combine fruit, ½ cup granulated sugar, juice and tapioca in **CROCK-POT®** slow cooker. Cover; cook on LOW 5 to 6 hours or on HIGH 2½ to 3 hours, or until fruit forms thick sauce.

2. Combine flour, 2 tablespoons granulated sugar, baking powder, and salt in medium bowl. Cut in butter using pastry cutter or two knives until the mixture resembles coarse crumbs. Whisk milk and egg in separate small bowl. Pour milk mixture into flour mixture. Stir until soft dough forms. Turn **CROCK-POT®** slow cooker to HIGH. Drop dough by teaspoonfuls on top of fruit. Sprinkle with brown sugar. Cover; cook 30 minutes to 1 hour or until toothpick inserted in dumplings comes out clean.

3. Sprinkle dumplings with additional brown sugar, if desired. Serve warm with ice cream, sweetened whipped cream or yogurt, if desired.

Makes 4 to 6 servings

Fresh Berry Compote

- 2 **cups fresh blueberries**
- 4 **cups fresh sliced strawberries**
- 2 **tablespoons orange juice**
- ½ **to ¾ cup sugar**
- 4 **slices (½ inch×1½ inch) lemon peel with no white pith**
- 1 **cinnamon stick** *or* **½ teaspoon ground cinnamon**

1. Place blueberries in **CROCK-POT®** slow cooker. Cover; cook on HIGH 45 minutes or until blueberries begin to soften.

2. Add strawberries, orange juice, ½ cup sugar, lemon peel and cinnamon stick. Stir to blend. Cover; cook on HIGH 1 to 1½ hours or until strawberries soften and sugar dissolves. Check for sweetness and add more sugar if necessary, cooking until added sugar dissolves.

3. Transfer **CROCK-POT®** stoneware insert from heating unit to heatproof surface to cool. Serve compote warm or chilled.

Makes 4 servings

Berry Bread Pudding

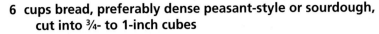

6 cups bread, preferably dense peasant-style or sourdough, cut into ¾- to 1-inch cubes
1 cup raisins
½ cup slivered almonds, toasted
6 eggs, beaten
2 cups packed brown sugar
1¾ cups milk (1% or greater)
1½ teaspoons ground cinnamon
1 teaspoon vanilla
3 cups sliced fresh strawberries
2 cups fresh blueberries
Fresh mint leaves (optional)

1. Coat **CROCK-POT**® slow cooker with nonstick cooking spray or butter. Place bread, raisins and almonds in bottom and toss to combine.

2. Whisk together eggs, brown sugar, milk, cinnamon and vanilla in separate bowl. Pour egg mixture over bread mixture; toss to blend. Cover; cook on LOW 4 to 4½ hours or on HIGH 3 hours.

3. Transfer **CROCK-POT**® stoneware insert from heating unit to heatproof surface. Allow bread pudding to cool and set before serving. Serve with berries and garnish with mint leaves, if desired.

Makes 10 to 12 servings

Pecan-Cinnamon Pudding Cake

- 1⅓ cups all-purpose flour
- ½ cup granulated sugar
- 1½ teaspoons baking powder
- 1½ teaspoons ground cinnamon
- ⅔ cup milk
- 5 tablespoons butter or margarine, melted, divided
- 1 cup chopped pecans
- 1½ cups water
- ¾ cup packed brown sugar
- Whipped cream (optional)

1. Coat **CROCK-POT®** slow cooker with nonstick cooking spray or butter. Combine flour, granulated sugar, baking powder and cinnamon in medium bowl. Add milk and 3 tablespoons butter; mix just until blended. Stir in pecans. Spread in bottom of **CROCK-POT®** slow cooker.

2. Combine water, brown sugar, and remaining 2 tablespoons butter in small saucepan; bring to a boil over medium heat. Pour over batter in **CROCK-POT®** slow cooker. *Do not stir.*

3. Cover; cook on HIGH 1¼ to 1½ hours or until toothpick inserted into center comes out clean. Let stand, uncovered, 30 minutes, then invert onto serving plate. Serve warm with whipped cream, if desired.

Makes 8 servings

Peach Cobbler

2 packages (16 ounces each) frozen peaches,
   thawed and drained
¾ cup plus 1 tablespoon sugar, divided
2 teaspoons ground cinnamon, divided
½ teaspoon ground nutmeg
¾ cup all-purpose flour
6 tablespoons butter, cut into small pieces
   Whipped cream (optional)

1. Combine peaches, ¾ cup sugar, 1½ teaspoons cinnamon and nutmeg in medium bowl. Place in **CROCK-POT®** slow cooker.

2. Combine flour, remaining 1 tablespoon sugar and remaining ½ teaspoon cinnamon in small bowl. Cut in butter with pastry blender or two knives until mixture resembles coarse crumbs. Sprinkle over peach mixture. Cover; cook on HIGH 2 hours.

3. Serve with whipped cream, if desired.

Makes 4 to 6 servings

Spiced Plums and Pears

2 cans (29 ounces each) sliced pears in heavy syrup, undrained
2 pounds red or black plums (about 12 to 14), pitted and sliced
1 cup packed brown sugar
1 teaspoon ground cinnamon
½ teaspoon ground ginger
¼ teaspoon grated lemon peel
2 tablespoons cornstarch
2 tablespoons water
Pound cake or ice cream (optional)
Whipped topping (optional)

1. Cut pear slices in half with spoon. Place pears, plums, brown sugar, cinnamon, ginger and lemon peel in **CROCK-POT**® slow cooker. Cover; cook on HIGH 4 hours.

2. Whisk cornstarch into water in small bowl until smooth. Stir into fruit mixture. Cook on HIGH until slightly thickened.

3. Serve warm or at room temperature over pound cake and garnish with whipped topping, if desired.

Makes 6 to 8 servings

Bananas Foster

12 bananas, cut into quarters
 1 cup flaked coconut
 1 cup dark corn syrup
⅔ cup butter, melted
¼ cup lemon juice
 2 teaspoons grated lemon peel
 2 teaspoons rum
 1 teaspoon ground cinnamon
½ teaspoon salt
12 slices pound cake
 1 quart vanilla ice cream

1. Combine bananas and coconut in **CROCK-POT®** slow cooker.

2. Stir together corn syrup, butter, lemon juice, lemon peel, rum, cinnamon and salt in medium bowl. Pour over bananas. Cover; cook on LOW 1 to 2 hours.

3. Arrange bananas on pound cake slices. Top with ice cream and warm sauce.

Makes 12 servings

Cherry Delight

1 can (21 ounces) cherry pie filling
1 package (about 18 ounces) yellow cake mix
½ cup (1 stick) butter, melted
⅓ cup chopped walnuts
   Whipped topping or ice cream (optional)

1. Place pie filling in **CROCK-POT®** slow cooker.

2. Mix together cake mix and butter in medium bowl. Spread evenly over pie filling. Sprinkle walnuts on top.

3. Cover; cook on LOW 3 to 4 hours or HIGH 1½ to 2 hours. Spoon into serving dishes. Serve warm with whipped topping or ice cream, if desired.

Makes 8 to 10 servings

Hot Fudge Cake

2 cups all-purpose flour
1¾ cups packed light brown sugar, divided
¼ cup plus 3 tablespoons unsweetened cocoa powder,
    divided, plus additional for dusting
2 teaspoons baking powder
1 teaspoon salt
1 cup milk
¼ cup (½ stick) butter, melted
1 teaspoon vanilla
3½ cups boiling water

1. Coat 4¼-quart **CROCK-POT**® slow cooker with nonstick cooking spray or butter. Mix flour, 1 cup brown sugar, 3 tablespoons cocoa, baking powder and salt in medium bowl. Stir in milk, butter and vanilla. Mix until well blended. Pour into **CROCK-POT**® slow cooker.

2. Whisk remaining ¾ cup brown sugar and ¼ cup cocoa in small bowl. Sprinkle evenly over mixture in **CROCK-POT**® slow cooker. Pour in boiling water. *Do not stir.*

3. Cover; cook on HIGH 1¼ to 1½ hours or until toothpick inserted into center comes out clean. Let stand 10 minutes, then invert onto serving platter or scoop into serving dishes. Serve warm; dust with additional cocoa powder, if desired.

Makes 6 to 8 servings

Peanut Fudge Pudding Cake

- **1 cup all-purpose flour**
- **1 cup sugar, divided**
- **1½ teaspoons baking powder**
- **⅔ cup milk**
- **½ cup peanut butter**
- **2 tablespoons vegetable oil**
- **1 teaspoon vanilla**
- **¼ cup unsweetened cocoa powder**
- **1 cup boiling water**
- **Chopped peanuts (optional)**
- **Vanilla ice cream (optional)**

1. Coat **CROCK-POT®** slow cooker with nonstick cooking spray or butter. Combine flour, ½ cup sugar and baking powder in medium bowl. Add milk, peanut butter, oil and vanilla. Mix until well-blended. Pour batter into **CROCK-POT®** slow cooker.

2. Combine remaining ½ cup sugar and cocoa in small bowl. Stir in boiling water. Pour into **CROCK-POT®** slow cooker. *Do not stir.*

3. Cover; cook on HIGH 1¼ to 1½ hours or until toothpick inserted into center comes out clean. Let stand 10 minutes, then invert onto serving platter or scoop into serving dishes. Serve warm with chopped peanuts and ice cream, if desired.

Makes 4 servings

Index

Metric Conversion Chart

VOLUME MEASUREMENTS (dry)

1/8 teaspoon	= 0.5 mL
1/4 teaspoon	= 1 mL
1/2 teaspoon	= 2 mL
3/4 teaspoon	= 4 mL
1 teaspoon	= 5 mL
1 tablespoon	= 15 mL
2 tablespoons	= 30 mL
1/4 cup	= 60 mL
1/3 cup	= 75 mL
1/2 cup	= 125 mL
2/3 cup	= 150 mL
3/4 cup	= 175 mL
1 cup	= 250 mL
2 cups = 1 pint	= 500 mL
3 cups	= 750 mL
4 cups = 1 quart	= 1 L

VOLUME MEASUREMENTS (fluid)

1 fluid ounce (2 tablespoons) = 30 mL
4 fluid ounces (1/2 cup) = 125 mL
8 fluid ounces (1 cup) = 250 mL
12 fluid ounces (1 1/2 cups) = 375 mL
16 fluid ounces (2 cups) = 500 mL

WEIGHTS (mass)

1/2 ounce	= 15 g
1 ounce	= 30 g
3 ounces	= 90 g
4 ounces	= 120 g
8 ounces	= 225 g
10 ounces	= 285 g
12 ounces	= 360 g
16 ounces = 1 pound	= 450 g

DIMENSIONS

1/16 inch	= 2 mm
1/8 inch	= 3 mm
1/4 inch	= 6 mm
1/2 inch	= 1.5 cm
3/4 inch	= 2 cm
1 inch	= 2.5 cm

OVEN TEMPERATURES

250°F	= 120°C
275°F	= 140°C
300°F	= 150°C
325°F	= 160°C
350°F	= 180°C
375°F	= 190°C
400°F	= 200°C
425°F	= 220°C
450°F	= 230°C

BAKING PAN SIZES

Utensil	Size in Inches/Quarts	Metric Volume	Size in Centimeters
Baking or Cake Pan (square or rectangular)	8×8×2	2 L	20×20×5
	9×9×2	2.5 L	23×23×5
	12×8×2	3 L	30×20×5
	13×9×2	3.5 L	33×23×5
Loaf Pan	8×4×3	1.5 L	20×10×7
	9×5×3	2 L	23×13×7
Round Layer Cake Pan	8×1½	1.2 L	20×4
	9×1½	1.5 L	23×4
Pie Plate	8×1¼	750 mL	20×3
	9×1¼	1 L	23×3
Baking Dish or Casserole	1 quart	1 L	—
	1½ quarts	1.5 L	—
	2 quarts	2 L	—